"Humankind has not woven the web of life.
We are but one thread within it.
Whatever we do to the web, we do to ourselves.
All things are bound together.
All things connect."
~ Chief Seattle, 1854 ~

Timber's Gambit

Nature's Guardians Series Book 2

Written and Illustrated
by
Alisha M. Risen-Kent

cover art by
Matthew Nixon

For more information, you can contact me at skydancer792007@yahoo.com or visit the Nature's Guardians website at https://www.naturesguardiansbookseries.com

Dedication

For my children, who are my strength, my motivation, my whole world.
My son, Gabriel, for his poem *Wolf*.
My parents, who always believed in my dream.
For *The Ocelot*, who helped me come up with many of the awesome ideas for this book.
Darryl, my beta, who caught all my mistakes.
Lastly, to my ROCK, Harker Heights United Methodist Church.
I can never say enough, how much my brothers and sisters in Christ have helped and encouraged me along the way.

Acknowledgements

I would like to thank all the people who helped me put this book together:
The Wolf Conservation Center for all their outstanding help and support. Without updated information on the status of the wolf and other predators, I would not have been able to stay true to my book.
The awesome people at P.A.W. You kept my spirits lifted among all the heartbreak with your breathtaking stories and pictures.
The Ian Somerhalder Foundation for information on environment conservation and great ways to become involved.
Wolf Angels for its beautiful pictures.
And lastly, the White Wolf Pack which provided me with amazing videos of wolves in action.

Wolf

(A Poem)

A pleasant creature
A beautiful coat
That you can find in the wild.
You think it's harmless
Maybe, but don't make it
MAD.
You'll wish you were dead
because of the pain
caused by the
bone crunching teeth.

His beautiful fur shines in
cold arctic snow but the smell
of blood nearby of a dead
deer and the howling
of a loner
the taste of meat
in his mouth

He can run up to 20
miles per hour in 10 feet
of freezing snow.

-Gabriel Kent

Table of Contents:

"Wolf": A Poem

Chapter One: The Pack   1

Chapter Two: My Father's Past   9

Chapter Three: The Hunt   23

Chapter Four: On My Own   38

Chapter Five: Swift   50

Chapter Six: Luke   63

Chapter Seven: Teamwork   73

Chapter Eight: Derby   83

Chapter Nine: Game of Chance   92

Chapter Ten: Gambit   103

Chapter Eleven: Captive   115

Chapter Twelve: Homeward Bound   125

Conservation Efforts   135

Sahara's Plight (excerpt)   141

Chapter One: The Pack

I was born into a large and boisterous family with two brothers and three sisters. My mother and father were the leaders of our pack. My father, a great alpha with obsidian fur, boasted that our pack was the largest in all the world. In my innocence, I believed him. My mother would sigh and roll her head, but my father would just puff out his chest and raise his chin.

At night, with the pack gathered around the den, it was easy to believe my father's claims. Dozens of my kin lay scattered over the rocky ledges, spilling into the valley below. This was my favorite time of day. One by one, they would lift their heads to the sky, starting with my father, and sing out a chorus to the stars. The tiny voices of me and my siblings were drowned out by the multitude, but I knew one day, I would sing louder than all the others.

My sister Zoe and I always engaged in fierce competition. I wouldn't admit it, but her strength exceeded mine. Our other siblings found humor in seeing me pinned beneath her. At least she didn't gloat as some of the older wolves did. In fact, she often tried to protect me against their bullying. One such case ended with the intervention of our father, and my ultimate shame.

"Just because you're bigger, Thor, it doesn't mean you can push Timber around," Zoe said, the hackles on her back raised into spikes. "Don't you know he is the heir to the pack? You should show some respect!"

The other wolf, a gangly sandy youth barely one turn of the seasons old, paused for a moment before throwing his head back and laughing. His friends, born in the same season, laughed with him.

"There is no way Timber's going to be alpha," he said, turning golden eyes on her.

"How can you say that?" she snapped. "He is directly descended from the greatest alpha in all the land. You're just jealous!"

Thor lunged at her, snapping his teeth inches from her nose. She whimpered on instinct and cowered to the ground, pulling her ears close to her head. Thor continued to snarl at her, flashing his teeth and growling low in his throat.

"You don't know anything, she-pup," he said, his voice low in warning. "Don't you know that most of the wolves in the pack are directly descended from

Zeus? Timber is just the most recent. The chances of him being the new alpha are slimmer than mine."

Regaining some of her courage, Zoe lifted her head. "If that is so, how come you have a better chance?"

"Because, sweet, innocent, naive Zoe, Zeus isn't my father. Nor is your mother mine."

Both Zoe and I gasped, understanding his meaning. Thor's mother had a forbidden meeting with a wolf outside of the pack. We weren't related in any way.

"Zeus could have banished my mother and abandoned us to the wilderness, but he pitied her. Lucky me."

He sat back on his haunches and raised his chin. I followed his example, not liking the way he looked down on me. His silent glare spoke of his resentment for me and my family. I couldn't understand where his hostility came from. Wasn't he grateful that father allowed them to stay in the pack, despite his mother's indiscretion?

"Know this, Timber," Thor continued, cocking his head to the side. "There is a long line of successors before you. If you really want to be an alpha, you are going to have to find a pack of your own. Zeus is not going to step down and even if he did, someone older than you will take his place."

"You mean, I have to leave?" I asked, horrified.

"Yes. I see Zeus' fire in you. This pack will not be able to tame the spark that is growing inside of you."

"But I don't want to leave."

"You will when you hear the moon calling to you."

"Stop it, Thor!" Zoe said, blocking me from his view. "Stop putting nonsense into his head."

"Well, as long as he has a girl to look after him, you don't have anything to worry about, Zoe," he said, getting to his feet.

"Wait a minute," I called, embarrassed. "I don't need her to protect me."

"Of course not."

Before I even realized what I was doing, I lunged at him, latching my tiny, needle-sharp teeth onto his leg. Thor howled, more in anger than pain. He reached down and grabbed me by my scruff. I released his leg and turned my head to snap at him, whining and growling at the same time. My mother was the only one to ever pick me up by my scruff and the indignity of Thor doing so was a blow to my pride. In his anger, he flung me away. I landed hard and rolled into a boulder, twisting my foot painfully. That was when my father came, alerted by my cries.

"Thor!" he bellowed.

The young wolf, as well as all those around him, coward low to the ground, some even turning onto their backs in submission. A high-pitched whimper issued from Thor and for one moment, I felt sorry for him. My father, head held high, towered over him, glaring down with his golden eyes.

"You dare attack a cub?" father said, his voice deceptively calm.

"No sir, I was only defending myself." Thor refused to look at my father, his gaze trained on the ground.

"Are you so weak to be threatened by a cub?"

"I'm sorry. It won't happen again."

"See that it doesn't."

"Yes, sir."

As soon as my father turned away, Thor and his followers fled for the trees. Father turned his disapproving glare onto me, and I shivered. With a sigh, he dropped his gaze and lowered his head. With the worst passed, I crawled to him on my belly, whimpering the whole way.

"Timber, are you all right, son?" he asked, nudging me with his nose.

"Yes, Father," I said, licking his nose.

"What am I going to do with you? I see so much of myself in you that it scares me."

He sighed again and laid down beside me. I snuggled into his fur for warmth and comfort.

"Stay clear of Thor. He is young and rash, and while I don't think he would really hurt you, it's better if you don't antagonize him."

"Antagonize?"

7

"Make him angry for no real reason."

"Yes, Father."

He glanced up at Zoe who sat a few feet away, staring at the place Thor had disappeared. Even from behind, I could tell she was still seething.

"Zoe," father called softly.

She turned her head around without moving the rest of her body. I noticed her body relax as she looked at us.

"Come here," he commanded.

She stood and turned around, loping over to us.

"I can't believe him!" she spouted, shaking her head.

"Don't think on it anymore," Father said, making room for her next to me.

My mind wandered from her and her outrage to the things Thor had said. Leave the pack? I would never see my family again. Did I want that? I pushed the troubling thoughts aside and tucked my nose into my father's fur.

Chapter Two: My father's Past

Several months passed as I grew into the wolf I would become, a copy of my father.   Instead of black fur, however, mine was silver. Even at half a year old, my large frame equaled that of our mighty alpha. It was whispered around the pack that I would grow larger and that perhaps, I did have a chance at becoming alpha.

I snarled at these comments, not wishing to take my father's place or dishonor him with their talk. My greatest tutor, Father taught me everything from pack etiquette to successful, and unsuccessful, hunting strategies. I asked him why he taught me both and he explained it to me.

"You see, Timber, if you know what doesn't work, you will avoid mistakes," he said. "In the time it takes to learn it on your own, you could starve."

"I understand. When will I be old enough to hunt with the pack?"

Father chuckled and shook his head. "So eager! Soon enough, son."

A few weeks later, I found myself sitting on the edge of the cliff that marked our den, staring down into the valley below. I watched as a huge deer sprang from the trees into a large clearing, followed closely by half of the pack. Fascinated, I followed the pack's maneuvers with my eyes. The deer was fast, faster than the pack, and I feared it would escape. Just as it reached the other side of the clearing, the rest of the pack, led by Father, shot forward. The spooked deer reared up, and Father lunged for it, taking it to the ground. I puffed out my chest, pride for him and our pack showing in my eyes.

Zoe, all long limbs and thick silver fur, sat next to me. She bumped my shoulder with hers and chuckled under her breath. I turned to her, feeling myself deflate.

"What?" I asked.

"You are Father's son," she said, looking out over the valley as well. "You just can't wait to join them."

"Neither can you," I said, teasing.

"You're right. So, why don't you say we go down and join them instead of sitting way up here observing?"

"You're the best sister ever."

"I know," she said, getting back to her feet and sauntering away.

I smirked and got to my feet as well. She's so full of herself! I thought. With her back turned, I lunged and pounced on her. My idea was sound; if she couldn't see me, I could finally pin her. Unfortunately, she knew my habits so well by now that she anticipated my attack. Before I could land a solid blow, she skipped out of the way. I hit the ground hard and tried to regain my footing, but she was faster and had me pinned beneath her large paws before I could get up.

"Give up, Timber," she said near my ear. "You will never be able to beat me."

"Alright, Zoe, you win. Now get off so we can eat."

She jumped off, laughing. I joined her. What else could I do? Together, we raced down the cliff to join the rest of the pack. The others made way for us. It had been that way ever since we could share in the hunt, the alphas and youngest ate first. After we had our fill, the rest of the pack took our place. Zoe and I, along with the rest of my youngest siblings, lounged away from the kill to digest our food. Not long after, Thor and his siblings joined us.

Thor and I had come to a truce of sorts. I stayed out of his way, and he stayed out of mine. Lately, though, the older wolf seemed to be more cordial than usual, almost friendly. Perhaps this was because I was bigger than him, even though I was younger. He plopped down next to me and smirked at the glare Zoe threw his way. Even though I had come to terms with Thor, she hadn't. I chuckled and she turned her glare to me.

"What?" I asked.

"Traitor," she said and laid her head on her paws.

I couldn't help it. I threw my head back and laughed. The other wolves around followed my lead and Zoe sulked next to me.

"It's alright, sister," I said to soothe her bruised ego. "It's better if we all get along."

She harrumphed, and I nudged her with my nose. Sighing, she turned to me and licked me.

"You're lucky you're my favorite brother." She turned and leaned her back against me, laying her head on my shoulder.

I just chuckled and laid my head down. By now, the rest of the pack were finishing their meal and picking their spots in the clearing to rest. I spotted our parents in the center, surrounded by the rest of the pack. They curled around each other, cleaning their faces as the sun slipped out of sight.

Father lifted his head and welcomed the night, his call echoing in the dusk. Others followed, each call adding to the others until everyone's voice could be heard. Zoe and I joined in the chorus, our songs finally loud enough to be heard amongst the others.

Far off in the distance, I could just barely hear the calls of another pack, their voices unfamiliar to me. It was rare that other packs were close enough to our territory to hear their calls. Father noticed as well, and his head turned in that direction. I felt a moment of trepidation. While we had not had any territory disputes in my young life, Father used to speak of them from his youth when he was just starting to build his pack. He told of vicious battles where not everyone walked away.

"Food is a precious commodity," he would tell us. "For you and your pack to survive, you must protect it, tooth and nail."

For a moment, I tried to imagine myself out there, on my own. It seemed like a lonely and frightening place, full of dangers I'd only imagined. Thor's words came back to me. Would I really want to leave the pack? Even to start my own family? I looked around at my kin laying around me. They all seemed content with the way things were. What made me so different?

As dusk turned to night, the pack rose to their feet and headed for the den. Zoe, sated and content, leaned on me most of the way. As strong as I was, it still proved a challenge to keep my feet with her pushing against me.

"Come on, Zoe," I said softly. "We're almost home."

She grumbled and stood on her own. I just shook my head and followed the rest of the pack. In front, I noticed Father searching the trees and clearings around us, his ears perked and body tense. Apprehension filled me, and I followed his gaze. Was there danger hiding in the trees? What could put my father, the great alpha, on alert? Mother, noticing his behavior, nudged his chin with her nose. They seemed to have a silent conversation, their eyes searching the other's.

As I watched, my father gave her a barely perceptible shake of his head, one I would have missed if I hadn't been watching so intently. She turned to look in the forest with him, her ears pulled against her head.

Some of the older wolves noticed their behavior and followed my parents' gaze, as alert as my father. My anxiety rose as I noticed mixed signals from the pack. While some were alert, many more looked afraid. Mother and Father, along with a handful of others, stopped as the rest of us continued. I wanted to join my father, but Zoe leaned against me again. If I stopped, she would fall.

Just as I passed Father, a flock of doves high above shot out of the trees, their wings beating out a wild staccato. Father flinched, something I'd never seen him do before, and Mother whined. He turned to her, finally relaxing, and licked her on her nose. She leaned against him, like how Zoe leaned against me, and I'm sure I heard her sigh. They rejoined the pack, and we continued toward the den. Once everyone was settled, and I had deposited Zoe off to bed, I approached Father.

"Timber, you should be resting," he scolded lightly.

"Is there a threat to the pack, father?" I asked without pause.

Father guided me off to the side, away from the others. "Why would you ask that?"

"I noticed you earlier...on the way back from the hunt. It seemed like you were looking for something. Also, I felt...frightened."

Father sighed and laid down, prompting me to do the same. "I think it's time I tell you my story."

He looked up at the sky and, although he seemed to be looking at the stars, I knew he was reliving the pain of a memory long past.

"I was barely older than you are now," he began. "My father led our pack as alpha, and my mother ruled alongside him. She was beautiful, with silver fur like you and Zoe. Zoe looks almost just like her. Our pack wasn't nearly as large as this one and we often quarreled with other packs over rights to hunt the land. But my father was a strong, cunning, and effective alpha. He secured his territory and kept us safe.

"When the seasons changed and the trees turned colors, a new threat came to our land. Two-legged hunters came baring sticks that were louder than thunder and hounds more vicious than bears. They laid traps that bit into our legs, keeping us from escaping.

"My father didn't know how to face this threat, so he did the only thing he could; he retreated deeper into the forest. This put us in clashes with other packs over ever-shrinking territory. In the end, it didn't matter. The hunters came for us all, despite what packs we belonged to. My mother hid me in a fox hole while she and the rest of the pack led the hunters away. That was the last I ever saw of them... any of them. Or the pack whose territory we had sought refuge in. They were all gone, and I was all alone.

"I wandered the forest for days until I found your mother, an orphan from another pack. Together, we traveled the land, picking up survivors here and there until eventually, we had a large pack of our own. We were all young, under two turns of the seasons, but together we prospered. The hunters have not returned for us, but I fear the day when they do. Sometimes our food supply is threatened, as they still come for the prey we eat."

My body shook next to my father, either from anger or fear, I couldn't tell. I couldn't imagine a creature that would kill so many of our kind for sport. What did these hunters gain by their slaughter?

"Be still, my son," Father said. "I have protected this pack for many turns of the seasons, and I will continue to do so until my last breath. Our territory is large, and there are places we can run to if they return."

I looked into my father's eyes, full of wisdom and courage, and believed him. Father cocked his head and seemed to be considering something before he turned back to me. I watched him, curious.

"I want you and your siblings to join in the hunt," he said. "It is time for you to learn how to work with the rest of the pack."

My excitement brought me to my feet, my tail wagging like a pup. "Yes, father! I'll tell them. Thank-you."

"Don't thank me," he chuckled. "It's a lot of work, and it takes patience, discipline, and teamwork. You and your brothers and sisters will team up with Thor."

Father watched me for a moment, probably expecting me to object. When I didn't, he continued.

"Listen to him, Timber. Thor may be rash at times, but he is an excellent hunter. You can learn a great deal from him."

"Yes, father. I will do as you say. Zoe may take some convincing, but I'm sure she'll come around."

"Good. I leave it to you. Now go get some rest."

I nodded and left, heading back to the den and my bed next to Zoe and my other siblings. I passed Mother on the way, and she nuzzled her head to mine for a moment, reinforcing our bond. When she pulled away, she nodded toward the den. I continued my way but stopped a moment later, turning to watch her as she headed toward my father. She laid down next to him, and he curled protectively around her. All the pack understood how unbreakable their bond was.

Some part of me wanted that for myself, but I knew the cost. I'd have to follow Thor's words and leave the pack. That kind of bond was reserved for pack leaders. For now, I was content with my siblings. I turned back and entered the den.

They were already asleep when I arrived, but I noticed Zoe crack her eye at my approach. She scooted over to make room for me, and I flopped down next to her. I decided to wait to tell her Father's news until morning. She laid her head on my back and yawned. Following her lead, I laid my head down as well. As excited as I was, I couldn't fight the sleep that overcame me.

Chapter Three: The Hunt

The next day, Thor met us just as we exited the den. A smirk stretched across his face as his gaze landed on Zoe. She turned up her nose and walked past him. I heard him chuckle and turn after her.

"Come on, Zoe," he said. "Don't be like that. Can't we let bygones be bygones?"

She stopped and turned to look at him. "Do you even know what a bygone is?"

Thor stopped as well and cocked his head to the side. "Well...no, not really."

Rolling her eyes, she walked away toward the creek near the den.

"She's a tough she-pup," Thor said as I came up next to him.

"Not a pup for much longer," I said as I watched him watch her. "And I don't think she will ever warm up to you. Too much buried hostility."

"Oh well. Are you ready to learn how to hunt?"

"Can't wait."

Father was right, Thor was an excellent hunter. We started off with small prey: rodents, birds, and lizards. Zoe, perfect as she was, excelled at it. Within a couple of days, she had mastered hunting small prey. Unfortunately, I was all limbs and couldn't catch a meal to save my life. At one point, I just laid down, frustrated, and watched everyone else.

Zoe's methods interested me and reminded me of a fox I once saw outside of our den. She stood very still, staring intently at a fallen tree. Her ears were perked and straight forward, and she cocked her head from side to side as though she could hear something no one else could. Suddenly, her head shot forward under the log, and she came out holding a ground squirrel. Lifting her head up, she opened her jaws, and the rodent disappeared down her throat.

From then on, I had no trouble catching food. Observing Zoe taught me all I needed to know. At least, when it came to small prey.

Several weeks after Thor began his training, he deemed us fit for a larger hunt. He and I had bonded over the course of my training. I think, perhaps, he gained a bit of respect for me. At the end of the day, we all sat together relaxing. Thor and I began to bond in a way I never thought possible. We were brothers and I knew if I ever needed him, he would be there for me. At the end of our training, he and I went together to see father. On the way, I noticed he seemed distracted, his mind on something other than hunting. Curious, I decided to ask what it was.

"Thor," I said, looking over at him. "Is something bothering you?"

"No," he answered too quickly. "Why do you ask?"

After our time together, I came to recognize certain cues from him. One of which was self-consciousness. This always happened when Zoe was nearby. Thor was an excellent, accomplished hunter but around Zoe, he was awkward and clumsy. Deep down I found it humorous and tried hard to keep my laughter to myself.

"You seem distracted," I said, answering his question. "In fact, you've been like that for a while now."

Thor stopped and sat on his haunches, a deep sigh leaving him. I stopped as well and joined him on the ground.

"I guess I couldn't hide it forever," he said, laying on his belly.

"Do you want to talk about it?"

"Timber, do you remember when I told you how one day, you would want a pack of your own?"

"Of course. That conversation is never far from my mind. It scared me half to death."

"What would you say if I told you that's what I wanted?"

"To scare me half to death?"

"No. A pack of my own."

I didn't know what to say. I sat dumbfounded. Why would Thor want his own pack? And it wasn't lost on me that he didn't say he wanted my father's pack.

"Why do you want your own pack?" I asked.

"Don't get me wrong, I love this pack. I love your family, both blood related and not. I couldn't ask for a better and more secure pack to belong to, and Zeus is like a father to me."

"I don't understand, Thor. Why do you want to leave then?"

"I crave a bond I can't get here. I'm almost two turns of the seasons old, and I feel something pulling me to seek it out. But..." he trailed off.

"But what?"

"I have bonds here as well. One specifically, that I don't want to lose."

"Which one is that?"

"Well...actually, it really isn't a bond because she hates me."

"Zoe?" I asked, jumping to my feet.

Thor got to his feet as well. What surprised me the most was his posture. His ears were pulled back, head cocked to the side, and tail tucked beneath him. He was submitting to me! I immediately backed down, unaware that I had been towering over him. Then, I did the only thing I could in that situation...I laughed. Thor stood straighter and looked at me like

I'd gone crazy. If wolves could flush from embarrassment, he would have.

"It isn't that funny," he pouted, returning to his seated position and turning away.

"Actually, it is!" I said, still chuckling. "Do you think staying here will gain Zoe's affection? Even if you did, you still couldn't claim her as your mate. Unless you took her with you when you left."

The silence that followed sobered me.

"Please tell me that's not what you intend?" I asked, cautious.

Another sigh left Thor as he got back to his feet. "Of course not," he said and trotted off.

Even though the conversation was over, it stayed on my mind long after. When we reached my father, I put it behind me.

"Hello, Thor. Timber," he said.

"Hello father," I said. Both Thor and I tipped our heads in respect.

"How goes the training?" Father asked Thor.

"Very well. I think they are ready to join the pack."

"Excellent! Tomorrow we will bring in a bison. It's been a week since the pack has fed well, and the two-legged hunters will be coming soon for the deer. I'd like one last big hunt before we move deeper into our territory where big game becomes scarce. Timber, we will need all the help we can get, so make sure you stick with Thor and follow what he says. This hunt is vital for our survival."

"Yes, sir."

"I will take care of him, Alpha. Timber did surprisingly well after the first couple of days."

Father seemed to stand a little taller at Thor's compliment. I knew then that he was proud of me. After a moment of reaffirming our bonds, we went our separate ways.

The next morning dawned bright and cold. A thin layer of frost coated the ground, and our breaths came out in puffs. Zoe, who stood next to me, was as excited about the day's hunt as I. Our other siblings gathered around us as we approached the spot where the rest of the pack was meeting. Thor noticed us and nodded his head once to tell us to sit next to him. Once seated, Father addressed the pack.

"We all know how important and how dangerous today's hunt is. Luckily, we have six more hunters to help bring down our prey. Everyone is essential, and everyone will have a specific role."

Father spent the next several minutes going over the best strategy. Most of my kin already knew the drill. I suspected my father had this meeting for the benefit of me and my siblings more than the need to actually strategize.

For our part, my siblings and I were to act as a wall to keep our prey from escaping. Father didn't want us near enough to get injured. I was a little disappointed, but I understood his reasoning. When the meeting concluded, we left as a pack down the cliff.

A herd of bison grazed, oblivious, in the field at the bottom of the valley. Great puffs of frosted air left their noses as they snorted and shook their heads. A few large calves intermingled near the center, frolicking among the older, more experienced females. On the edge of the field was a wide river, vapor rising from it in the early morning air. A heavy fog rolled down the mountain into the valley and I knew before long, it would obscure our line of sight.

Father, and a handful of others, moved off toward the far side of the field. Thor directed us to follow him as he went the opposite direction. Now, I understood. The pack was surrounding the herd from all sides. We would leave a small opening for most of the herd to escape through while we focused on a specific one to take down. Just before the fog reached us, I heard my father's howl. It was his call to action, and we responded, letting him know we were all in place. The herd, hearing our calls, panicked, and charged for the river.

As one, the pack lunged out of hiding, closing the circle around the herd. The bison stomped and bellowed, making the ground beneath our feet tremble. I knew right away which one my father had singled out. It was an old male, slower than the rest but still full of power and fire. He bellowed his rage and shook his head at the pack, his sharp horns and hooves brandished in warning.

As planned, we allowed the rest of the herd to escape across the river. But they did not flee. Instead, they turned, torn between fleeing or rescuing their doomed family member. The pack kept a wary eye on them. It was not uncommon for the herd to charge the pack.

The captured bull continued to bellow, his angry cries echoing through the valley. He stomped the ground and spun from one side to the other, trying to keep his eyes on the pack that surrounded him. Father had not yet given the signal to attack, and I wondered why. The beast was obviously trapped and there were plenty of us to take him down. In my naivety, I thought the others were over-cautious. I decided to make the first move but just as I moved, Thor snarled.

"What are you doing, pup?" he hissed. "It's too dangerous right now. That bull will gore you."

Thor's lack of confidence angered me, but I stepped back anyway. I noticed the concerned look in Zoe's eye and felt embarrassment flood through me. After several more minutes of parading around the bull, his exhaustion caught up to him and he collapsed to his knees. This was the moment I'd been waiting for. Without waiting for the rest of the pack, I lunged like I had seen my father do so many times before.

In the back of my mind, I heard Thor and Zoe yell. But I was too distracted by the bull in front of me to heed their warning, the bull that was suddenly back on his feet.

To me, everything that happened next was in slow motion, even though I knew only a few seconds had passed. The bull tipped his head and rammed it into my chest, the horns miraculously missing me. With a thrust of his powerful neck, he flung me into the air. The pack below me barked and howled, the sound hollow in my head. Just as I hit the ground, time sped up again.

I winced at the pain of a rock tearing through my side. Before I could regain my feet, the bull was on me. His sharp hooves tore at the ground, narrowly missing me. I struggled to my feet and snapped at him, latching onto his nose. The pack came to my aid, then, snapping and tearing at the bull.

But the bull had allies as well. The herd returned with a vengeance, chasing the pack off. The bull was still focused on me, roaring in rage. He swept his head around and threw me off. I landed a few feet away on my bruised ribs. In the distance, I could hear the pack howling. They were scared for me.

From the corner of my eye, I saw Zoe leap out ahead of the pack, determined to come to my aid. The bull blocked my view of her, his dark eyes boring into me. For a few seconds, we just stared at each other. Then, beyond all reason, he turned and stampeded off with the rest of the herd. I collapsed as the adrenaline drained from me and left me exhausted.

"Timber!" Zoe cried, rushing up to me. "Are you alright?"

I couldn't lift my head to greet her. In fact, all I could do was whine pitifully.

"Stupid, stupid, Timber!" she continued, resting her nose under my neck. "I can't believe you did that. Do you have any idea how scared I was?"

"Sorry," I choked out.

"Are you hurt?"

"Just a little. But I think my pride is damaged beyond repair."

"Good. You could use some humility."

I struggled to my feet and winced from the pain in my side. As the pack parted and my father approached me, I knew I was in trouble. Ignoring my pain, I fell to the ground on my back, my ears close to my head, and whimpered. Father towered over me, his golden eyes boring into mine. I wanted the ground to open and swallow me. But it didn't. After several minutes of tense silence, he sighed and closed his eyes.

"Are you alright, son?" he asked.

"Yes, father," I squeaked.

"Go rest. Once we take down the bison, I'll call for you."

I nodded and slipped off into the cover of the forest. Zoe watched me, pain crossing her eyes. I knew it hurt her to see me reprimanded. Father was the only one she couldn't protect me from. At a gentle nudge from Thor, she turned and followed the pack.

Chapter Four: On My Own

Eventually, the pack brought down a deer. I heard my father's call from a great distance away just as the sun was setting. I struggled to my feet and lumbered in that direction. Every few minutes, Zoe would howl. I knew she worried for me; I could hear it in her voice. The longer it took for me to reach them, the more anxious she became. Ignoring the pain in my side, I began to trot.

The sun had long set by the time I reached them. Zoe ran up to me, whining and licking my face. Her enthusiastic welcome momentarily distracted me from the disapproving stares of the rest of the pack. Thor came up next. Although he didn't greet me as Zoe did, he did tip his head at me.

"Welcome back, pup," he said. "We saved you some."

"Thanks, Thor. I'm sorry about earlier."

"Well, what's done is done."

Zoe led me to a spot away from everyone else and showed me the piece she had hidden. It wasn't much bigger than a rabbit and I sighed.

"Sorry, Timber," she said sitting next to me. "The deer wasn't big enough for us to eat a lot. This is all I could save."

"It's alright, Zoe. It'll be fine. I'm lucky to even get this after my blunder."

Thor joined Zoe and I, laying down close to her. I finished my meal and rested against her. Just as I was dozing off, Father approached us. My eyes were closed so I didn't notice at first. Zoe nudged me and I lifted my head.

"Timber," he said. "Come walk with me."

I struggled to my feet, my legs shaking with the effort. Father waited patiently until I could support my weight enough to move. Then, he led me off toward the edge of the pack. Once we were alone, he sat down and stared out over his territory.

"My responsibilities are great," he began. "I must ensure that there is enough food for our family and that our home stays safe from hunters, predators, and other wolves. I must continually reinforce our boundaries. To do this, I need every member of the pack to follow their role exactly. Everyone must be in sync with everyone else, especially with a pack as big as ours. Do you understand what this means?"

"Yes, Father. It means I messed up. I didn't do what you said, and we lost an important meal. I could see the disappointment in the others."

"Timber, I knew when you were just a pup that this pack would not be enough for you. You had too much spirit, too much fire to simply follow someone else. You are not the only one. In the beginning, we lost many young males to that fire. They felt the calling and left to create packs of their own. Our nearest rival is one of those males. Fenrir was part of my pack in the beginning. When he left, there was no animosity. It's just the way of things. You will be the same."

"But father. I don't want to leave."

"Not yet perhaps. But you will. In a few months, maybe a full turn of the seasons, this pack will no longer meet your needs."

"Zoe needs me, as well as my other siblings. And I need them. How could I leave when we need each other?"

"Timber, there is a difference between needing and relying on each other. In time, you will understand the difference. Think on that. One day, I shall hear the calls of your own pack echoing through that valley and those ice capped mountains. On that day, my heart will burn warmer than the noon sun in summer, for I shall be the proudest father in all the land."

I looked out over the valley like he had done just moments before, trying to imagine a world without my family; a world with one of my own.

The following months were both hard and plentiful. Father led us deeper into his territory where the two-legged hunters rarely ventured. Before long, snow covered the ground and the bitter cold caused ice to form on my nose and between my toes. Hunting proved fruitful. The deer made for easier prey and the bear that competed with us were nowhere to be found. When I asked my father about this, he said they slept the whole winter.

Thor and Zoe seemed to grow closer, and she spent more time with him than she did me. Even my father seemed to distance himself. Or perhaps it just seemed that way to me. It was as if, day by day, I moved further and further away. As if I were still the spectator pup of my youth. Each day brought further distance, until all at once I was apart from them. When the seasons changed again, I knew something inside me had changed.

At a year old, I dwarfed my father and everyone else in the pack. My silver fur glistened in the light of the moon and my golden eyes pierced deep into the darkness. My paws left huge tracks in my wake. I would often find myself wandering off from the pack without even realizing it. Hours would pass before I noticed I'd slipped away.

When my new siblings came into the world, a brother and three sisters, I knew it was time for me to leave. My father, noticing my resolve, took me aside for the last time, leading me up a rise overlooking the pack.

"Are you ready, Timber?" he asked.

"I think I am. The wind calls to me, and I am ready to listen."

"What of your bonds here?"

I sat down and stared off into the distance. That was the hard part. I would miss my family, and I couldn't deny some trepidation at setting off on my own. I answered my father as truthfully as I knew how.

"I will always carry the bonds I have made," I said looking back to him. "You, Mother, Zoe...even Thor. In my heart, I will always cherish these bonds."

Father closed his eyes for a moment and bowed his head. An expression I'd never seen before crossed his face but was gone when he opened his eyes again.

"Before you go, I want to tell you a few things of great importance. First, keep clear of other territories. Alphas have been known to kill lone wolves who trespass in their territory. Listen for the calls among packs and don't get too close. Second,

44

try to stay deep in the forest. Bears and mountain lions can be a problem if you don't pay attention but it's better than the two-legged hunters.

"Keep a watchful eye out for the hunters. They are ruthless and cunning. They hunt with thunder sticks that can kill from a long distance away. They also use traps that they bury in the ground. If you step on one, you won't be able to get out. Their hounds are loud and viscous and will flush you out of hiding, straight toward the hunters."

I squirmed uncomfortably. Father noticed and stood in front of me, making sure he had my attention.

"This is very important, Timber," he continued. "The two-legs live in our territories as well. You will likely encounter their dwellings. Do not go near them. They are temptations, easy sources of food and shelter. Even if it seems like there is no danger, there is. Like I said, the two-legs are cunning, and they don't like us coming near their dens. If you follow this advice, you should do just fine."

"Thank-you, Father."

"You are my greatest accomplishment, my son, and I always knew you wouldn't stay here long."

"I'm going to miss you. And Zoe. Speaking of Zoe, I think Thor may leave soon as well. Perhaps even taking her with him."

A smile drew across my father's face. "I am the pack's alpha. Very little escapes my watchful eyes. I know most intentions before they even realize it. Be sure to say your good-byes to your mother before you leave, Timber."

"I will, Father."

I turned and loped down the rise, making my way to my mother's den, where my youngest siblings slept. Just outside, I called for her. A moment later, she emerged, tired but content. I nuzzled her neck with my nose before stepping back.

"I'm leaving, Mother," I said. "I've come to say good-bye."

She reached up and licked my chin. "Take care of yourself, Timber. And call home every now and again."

I thought of the incident several months before when the rival pack answered our call after our hunt and the story my father told of its alpha. Was he "calling home"?

"I'm going to miss you," she said, rubbing up against me.

"I'm going to miss you, too. But the little ones should keep you busy for a while."

"That's true. Be safe."

"I will." With one last nuzzle, I turned and headed for the edge of the clearing.

I debated seeing Zoe one last time. I would miss her more than anything. Thinking it best for both of us, I decided against it, and, with a wide trot, I disappeared into the trees. Several minutes later, I heard the unmistakable sound of running paws. I'd just turned around when Zoe plowed into me, slamming me to the ground.

"You...You…, Ugh!" she stammered, pinning me beneath her. I could have dislodged her, but I waited for her to burn off her anger. "Were you just going to leave without saying good-bye?"

"Actually, I was planning on calling back to you when I was too far away to be followed," I said.

"You're hopeless, Timber." She laid across me, and I rolled over. Thor appeared behind her, smiling. "And I'm really going to miss you."

"Me, too, pup," I said, fighting to hide my smile.

"Timber, we're not pups anymore." She seemed to be reminding herself as much as me.

"Yeah, I know," I said with a sigh. She rolled off, and I stood up, looking over at Thor. "Take care of my sister, friend."

"Of course," he said. "Just take care of yourself out there. I hope you find what you're looking for."

"Wait a minute," Zoe said, looking between us. "Why does Thor have to take care of me? I can take care of myself."

"All in good time, Zoe," I said, turning from her. "All in good time."

With that, I took off running, my long legs stretching as I flew over the ground. The wind whipped through my fur and buzzed in my ears, but I didn't stop. Something was calling to me, and I was determined to find out what it was. Suddenly, I heard Zoe's howl, followed closely by Thor. They were telling me farewell. Soon, the rest of the pack joined in until the whole forest echoed their call. My heart squeezed at the sentiment. I could only hope to have a pack as close as that one.

Chapter Five: Swift

I traveled several hours to reach my father's border. I knew once I crossed that boundary, marked with my parent's unmistakable scent, there would be no turning back. With a deep breath, I crossed over.

I was now in the no-man's land between my father's territory and that of his closest rival. Traveling through this neutral zone, I went in search of a territory I could call my own. It wasn't long before I found trouble, or should I say, trouble found me.

The neutral zone is a thin strip of land nestled between rival wolf packs. Generally, the packs don't cross into it, preferring to stick to their well-marked boundaries. On rare occasions, though, when a hunt is essential, they will follow their prey into the neutral zone. Wolf packs who do this are at risk of being attacked by rival packs as they move too close to the borders. My father used to tell me stories where this happened. In one case, a small pack was attacked, and their alphas killed. With the rest of the pack being young wolves, my father suspected they were unable to survive on their own.

Game in the neutral zone, both large and small, is scarce and crossing the border into another wolf's territory to search for it is risky. However, Thor and Zoe taught me how to hunt on my own, even against seemingly insurmountable odds. As I made my way through, always on alert, I took note of several different tracks scattered along the forest floor. Most of these were rodents: rabbits, squirrel, and mice. I also noticed the long-fingered tracks of the masked creature my father called a raccoon. The most recent tracks, however, belonged to a creature very similar to me.

While they were smaller than mine, they were bigger than those of a fox. I searched my brain for any memory of what this creature may be. Would they compete with me for the limited prey found in the neutral zone? I scanned the trees for any sign of it, but the forest was quiet. My stomach grumbled. I had to find food. Dismissing the mysterious tracks for now, I lowered my nose and picked up the scent of a rabbit.

I followed the tracks for several minutes before I found my prey. Being downwind, the rabbit was unaware of my presence. A cautious creature by nature, it kept lifting its head to take account of its surroundings, its long ears swiveling around its head. I waited for my moment. When it dropped back down into the long grass, I leapt over the log I hid behind and pounced on the unsuspecting creature. The attack was over before it even had time to register what had happened. I took my meal to a quiet nook beneath some overhanging boulders.

Along the way, I felt something watching me. I kept looking around, trying to locate the source of my anxiety. If it were another wolf, or worse, a wolf pack, I'd have a hard time escaping. Nothing seemed out of the ordinary. The birds were even chirping away in the trees, undisturbed. I dismissed my worries and settled down to eat. Before I could savor my food, a noise to my right caught my attention. It was too big to be a rodent. I stood up and turned in that direction, a low growl rumbling in my chest.

I waited a full minute, staring into the brush. Still nothing. Relaxing, I turned back around to my meal. To my dismay, it was gone. I just barely caught sight of a very wolf-like tail disappearing on the other side of the boulders. I charged after it, my hunger making me careless. The creature, whatever it was, weaved through the trees and brush with agility and speed. I found it hard to keep up, even though I was nearly twice its size.

Several minutes after the chase began, the creature jumped onto a boulder and turned to me. Before I could reach it, my meal disappeared down its throat. A coyote! Now it all made sense. Father had warned me about these cunning tricksters. They were thieves and would steal your meal if you let them.

I growled from hunger and anger. "You owe me a meal, thief!" I snapped.

The coyote laughed and ran off. Without thinking, I gave chase. It was fast, and it knew the territory well. After a few minutes, I realized I would never catch it and stopped my pursuit.

"Go on, then," I yelled, panting from exertion.

In answer, I heard the coyote cackle, its dog-like bark echoing through the forest.

"Done already?" he asked, although I couldn't pinpoint his exact location. His laughter echoed through the trees.

Preferring to ignore the nuisance, I turned around and trotted off to find a new meal.

"Aww, come on. Don't leave yet," he continued. "I was havin' so much fun!"

I turned my head toward the sound and there he was, not fifteen feet from me. A smile stretched across his narrow snout and his eyes sparkled with mischief. My stomach grumbled, reminding me of my hunger.

"I don't have time to play with you," I said. "*Somebody* stole my meal."

"Not I," he said, a look of false indignation crossing his face. "Tha' rabbit was jes' layin' there. If it were yur's, ya should'a eaten it."

I bit back my anger. "Get lost, pest. I have to find something else to eat."

"Aww... yu'r fun when yu'r angry" he said, daring to come closer to me. "And my name isn't Pest. It's

Swift-tail. But, since we're friends, you can call me Swift."

"We are not friends, *pest*. Go on."

"How rude! I'll remember you!" He turned and jumped onto a boulder. Before running off, he turned back around and cocked his head as though he had forgotten something. "By the way...what's yur name?"

I sighed, exasperated. "Timber. Now go away."

"See ya later, Timbah."

I really hope not, I thought.

Swift flicked his tail in a circle, turned, and ran off laughing into the brush. I shook my head. I had a feeling that I'd be seeing him again. Picking up the trail of a ground squirrel, I followed it, my stomach grumbling the whole way.

The next day, I woke up hungry. With only small prey, I'd have to hunt more often. I took a quick look around. No sign of Swift. Or much else for that matter. The neutral zone was an eerie place. Growing up in my father's pack, I was used to noise:

other wolves, bison in the fields, or elk bellowing through the trees. But in the neutral zone, all was quiet. Sure, I could hear birds high up in the trees, but little else. I shook off the uneasy feeling and got to my feet. Time to find breakfast.

By mid-day, my hunger was somewhat sated, mostly on the few mice I found skittering through the undergrowth. I traveled quite some distance in my search for food and, with a mostly full belly, decided to take a nap. A large, flat boulder lying fully in the sun called out to me. Trotting over to it, I laid down and stretched out my limbs. Ah, what bliss! Just as I closed my eyes, a noise reached my ears. I sighed, exhausted from the days' previous endeavors.

"'ello, Timbah," Swift called, too close to my ear. I jumped up and glared at him.

"I don't have anything for you to steal today so-"

"Oh, I know that. I jes' wanted to come say 'ello to my new friend." He plopped down next to me.

"Swift, we're not friends. Now go find your own rock." I laid my head down on my paws and closed my eyes.

"Nah, I think I like this one." He rolled over onto his side and rested his head on my back.

I sighed and struggled to my feet, dislodging Swift's head. "Fine. I'll go find another rock."

"Okay, see ya later."

I turned to scowl at the nuisance, but Swift wasn't even looking at me. He had stretched out on my rock with a gaping yawn. I shook my head and turned back toward the trees. Time to move on anyway.

The next few days were relatively peaceful, and blissfully Swift-free. I'd moved quite far from my home territory, but I could still hear my family in the distance. Unfortunately, I could also hear the rival pack. And they were much closer. I moved with caution while hunting, always aware that danger could be lurking in the shadows.

By nightfall, my trepidation took more of my attention than my prey. The birds were silent. Too silent. I peered into the darkness, trying to find the source of my unease. My eyes, like all wolves, pierced through the shadows, glowing in the night as they reflected the light of the moon. For a time, the night was quiet and still. A movement in the undergrowth caught my attention, and I turned to it. A rabbit! The rodent had its eyes pinned to something ahead of it, its long ears swiveling back and forth.

Had I not been so hungry, I probably would have paid closer attention to where the rabbit was looking. But hunger does funny things to the mind. My thoughts were solely on filling my stomach. I launched out at it, surprised when I landed square on its back.

Before I could enjoy my easy catch, however, a chorus of growls greeted me from the shadows at the same place the rabbit had been looking. I stood, frozen with the rabbit in my jaws for a moment too long. The pack, or at least part of it, came down on me, growling and snapping. There were three of them, all males, and thankfully, all smaller than me.

"What are you doing in our territory, rogue?" the biggest of the three asked.

"This territory doesn't belong to anyone," I cried, trying to defend my back.

"Wrong! All this land belongs to our alpha, Fenrir."

A chill ran down my spine at the name. Fenrir was one of the wolves who broke off from my father's pack in the beginning, his closest confidante and friend. Now, he and his pack were our closest and strongest rival.

"I'm just passing through," I said, lowering myself to the ground.

"We don't take kindly to pups who steal from our land."

Before I could defend myself, two of the males pounced on me while the third lifted his head and howled. I knew I was in trouble. If I didn't escape from these three, the rest of the pack would come to help. As big as I was, there was no way I would be able to fight off a whole pack. I turned my head and locked my jaws on the leg of the smallest male. He yelped and released his hold on me. Then I turned my attention to the second male.

The fight that followed was short and brutal and would leave me forever scarred with a piece of my ear missing. After several minutes of slashing claws and snapping jaws, I managed to wiggle free of their hold and sprinted into the dense foliage, my tail tucked between my legs. Even with their extensive injuries, I heard them pursue me. A howl, far too close, echoed eerily through the darkness, and I knew the rest of the pack were catching up.

I scanned my surroundings looking for a place to hide. With my injuries, I wouldn't be able to outrun them for long. As I leapt over a fallen tree, I glanced behind me. There! A hidden hollow. I turned back and scrambled into the hole, just big enough for my large body to squeeze through. My chest heaved as I tried to catch my breath, and the sound roared in my ears. I strained to hear past my breathing and out into the forest.

For a moment, I couldn't hear anything except the pounding of my heart. Then I heard it, the thunder of paws on the ground above me. Too many! Shortly after, the silhouettes of wolves passed over my hiding place and continued into the night.

For the rest of the night, I remained alert, in case the pack came back. I cleaned my wounds and tried to get a little rest. Just before dawn, a noise snapped me out of my half-sleep. The owner of the burrow had returned.

Chapter Six: Luke

At the sound of scraping near the burrow
entrance, my head shot up. A dark body was
ambling toward me, not yet aware of my presence. A
sense of panic overcame me, and before I could think

about my actions, I growled. The animal froze and snorted.

"Oy! Who's invaded my home?" the animal growled, puffing up his body.

"I'm sorry," I said, trying to get to my feet in the tight quarters. "I'll leave right away."

"Darn right, ya will! Go on, get outta here!" The animal didn't seem to realize that I couldn't squeeze past him. "Well...go on now. Off with ya!"

"Umm...could you make room?"

"Of all the..." he grumbled as he turned and backed out of the burrow.

"I'm really very sorry, sir," I said as I pushed out after him.

The animal was a badger and by the expression on his face, he was less than thrilled by my overnight occupation of his home. I glanced quickly around the trees looking for Fenrir's pack, but there was no sign of them. Even the animals were at ease, birds singing in the trees and squirrel dashing across branches. I turned my attention back to the irate badger.

"Do ya often steal other folks' homes?" the old codger asked.

"No, sir. I just needed a place to hide for a while."

The badger perused my still-healing wounds and torn ear. "Looks like they did a number on ya. Normally, I'd whip the fur off ya, but it looks like someone else has done that already."

"That they did." I collapsed onto my belly, exhausted from the chase, the sleepless night, and hunger. "They weren't even supposed to be here. I've been very careful to stay in the neutral zone."

"Well, that wolf pack has been moving beyond its territory for a while now. Food has become scarce and they're getting desperate."

"I don't understand. Fenrir's pack is nearly as big and strong as my father's."

"It's those two-legs. They're chasing folks from their homes, deeper into the forest where they clash with other territories. Two-legs also eat the same things we do. They don't like it when we eat their food. Lately, I've noticed bait traps that lure deer away from their natural routes. The two-legs been setting up dens on that pack's land, pushin' them, and everything else, further into the forest."

"That's terrible. How can I find a territory of my own when other pack lines are moving?" My stomach chose that moment to grumble.

"Not really my problem." The badger moved down into the burrow and disappeared.

A mouse caught my attention a few feet away. I needed a real meal but at that moment, I was too weak to hunt anything bigger. I got to my feet and went to chase the rodent down. It was fast, too fast for me, and I sat and stared forlornly at the hole it disappeared into. A sigh from the badger's burrow had me turning my head in that direction. He was laying just at the edge of the entrance watching my pitiful attempt.

"Ya keep up that way and yu're gonna starve," he said. "Ya have to conserve yur energy. Even if yu're ignorant tail does manage to catch that mouse… do ya really think it's worth all that energy? Ya have a lot more to worry about than yur own territory."

"I was doing just fine until someone started stealing my food," I defended. "Now, I'm too weak to hunt."

The badger sighed again and got to his feet. "Up that hill there are rabbit holes, I can dig em out, they run into you. Then when ya send them to ground I'll be waiting. We both eat… Got it, pup?"

"Why would you do that?"

"Because I can't catch them out in the open and frankly, I'm tired of eating bugs."

"Alright. I suppose two is better than one. But you should know, I'm being tailed by a coyote."

"Yep, that would be Swift-tail. Don't worry, he's stolen a meal from me once, too." Stretching, he yawned and left the burrow. "What's yur name, pup?"

"Timber." I tried not to show my irritation at being called 'pup'.

"Timber? What kinda name is that.... oh, never mind. I'm Luke, now let's get a move on before ya starve, and I'll have to eat ya."

"Thank-you, I think."

Luke loped past me, grumbling under his breath. "Meh... whatever."

The badger's method worked well, and I ate better than I had since first leaving my father's pack. Before the sun had reached its apex, I was sated and full. I followed Luke back to his burrow but not inside, instead lounging in the sun a few feet from the entrance. All was quiet and for a few moments, I forgot about the dangers hiding in the trees. I'd only been asleep for a short time, however, when a familiar, nagging feeling roused me. I reluctantly opened one eye and was greeted with the smiling face of Swift, much too close to mine.

"'ello, Timbah," he said. "How ya been? Looks like ya lost a fight. Do ya want me to clean it for ya?"

"Ugh," I grumbled, rolling away from him.

"Well, tha's not very nice. Come on, lemme 'elp. I'm an expert at cleanin' up scrapes. Why, this one time..."

I rolled my head in Swift's direction, hoping that my death glare would discourage him from annoying me. But the coyote wasn't even looking at me. He sat a few feet away, engrossed in his own storytelling, which I had chosen to ignore. Realizing it would be a long story, I laid my head back down, effectively dismissing him.

"...and so then, the farmer's mate waved tha' wooden stick at me, striking me on the head while I ran off with one of those chickens. I'd ne'er seen a human tha' shade of color before. Man was she mad-," Suddenly, Swift interrupted his tale, probably realizing that I hadn't heard a word of it. "Are you even listenin'? I'm trying to teach ya a valuable lesson here."

Yawning, I rolled over onto my feet. "Really, Swift? And what lesson would that be?"

"Why, how to properly steal a chicken, o' course." He seemed shocked by my question.

"Have you ever thought about not stealing from 'humans' at all? Maybe then your brain wouldn't be damaged by so many blows."

Swift cocked his head, seeming to consider my statement. "Nope! I don' mind a few blows if it means a free meal."

"Swift, have you ever considered hunting like everyone else? You know, instead of stealing from everyone?"

"Why on earth would I do tha'? It's much easier to find 'discarded' food. I mean, look a' me. You don' look this good by wastin' energy huntin'." He flicked his full tail around in circles to emphasize his point.

"You're hopeless. And you're going to get yourself killed one day."

"Naw, I'm too fast to get caught. I've already lived six winters and plan to live for a whole lot more."

"Then, you need to come up with a better strategy." I got to my feet and stretched. It was still several hours until nightfall, and I didn't want our conversation to wake Luke. "By the way, what is a 'human'?"

"You call them two-legs, or hunters."

I stopped and stared after the coyote. "You went into the hunters' land?"

"Yeah, do it all the time."

"Swift, that's dangerous!"

"Not if ya know what yu're doing."

"You know what, I was right. You are brain damaged."

"Keep telling yourself tha', pup. At least I have a full belly." With a flick of his tail, he dashed off and disappeared into the trees. For one annoying moment, I feared for him.

Shaking my head, I pushed the feeling aside. It was time to explore my surroundings. With pack lines moving, an opportunity to claim my own territory opened. I just needed to claim it first. This part of the neutral zone seemed promising. Game, although not large, was plentiful. The hill that Luke had taken me to offer a high vantage point to look out over the surrounding territory. Not too far away was an open field. I knew it was near another pack's territory, but it offered the best option for large game. Right now, lush green grass and wildflowers filled the meadow.

In the hopes of finding big prey, I headed for it. The hike took most of the afternoon. By the time I reached the meadow, the sun rested just above the horizon, streaking purples and oranges across the sky. I picked up the scent of a deer from a few days before and followed it.

Hidden in the long grass of the meadow was a crystal-clear lake. I looked back at the tree line just a few yards away. This would be the perfect spot for an ambush. I committed the spot to memory and headed back to Luke. If I were lucky, I'd be able to bring down a deer soon.

Chapter Seven: Teamwork

The following week, Luke and I formed a close hunting relationship. Although still irritable, he seemed to appreciate both my help and my companionship. We ate well, if only a little at a time, and I grew comfortable and relaxed. The meadow proved my favorite place, although I never found the elusive deer. Off in the distance, mountains rose tall and formidable, their peaks forever tipped in snow. It was a constant reminder that summer could end at any moment

For now, a gentle breeze drifted down and across the tall grasses and still lake. The deceptively calm water looked solid enough to walk across. Occasionally, an eagle or osprey would fly over, swoop down, and break the illusion by snagging a fish near the surface. I spent most of my days there. In fact, Luke often had to come fetch me when he was ready to hunt.

One afternoon, a few weeks after claiming the meadow as my own, a subtle shift in the winds alerted me to the changing seasons. Luke retired to his burrow, and I took my most recent meal to my favorite resting place. The rabbit wasn't large, nor was I overly hungry, but I needed to build up a reserve of energy. A gust of arctic air blew through the meadow, throwing up puffs of dandelions.

Leaving my rabbit safely ensconced under a branch, I stepped out into the open. The tops of the trees on either side of the meadow swayed and shook, their leaves falling like snow.

"I'm running out of time," I said to no one in particular.

I had wanted to establish my pack before winter set in. Hunting large prey was most successful in late winter, but it would be difficult alone. I turned back and crawled under my makeshift den to finish my meal. As I moved the branch, I already knew my rabbit was gone.

"Thanks for the meal, Timbah!" Swift said as he ran off, his mouth full of my dinner.

I sighed. *Well, at least he'll enjoy it,* I thought. Curling into a ball, I tucked my nose under my tail and fell asleep.

Over the next few weeks, winter hit with a vengeance. Snow drifted down from the mountains and ice formed on the edges of the lake. The leaves on the trees changed color from green to brilliant reds, yellows, and oranges. It was like sunset had fallen on them and I marveled at their beauty. Our prey was adapting as well. Rabbit and squirrel were busy collecting food for winter and I had to work harder to chase them down.

The wintery mix of ice and snow played havoc with my feet. The ground was not yet frozen, so the moisture created a muddy slush that stuck between my toes. After a week of hunting through mud and thick leaf litter, it became obvious we would need a new strategy.

Several days later, Luke ambled toward his burrow. Another day without a kill. Our food source was either running thin or it had caught on to our game. Three days without food left both of us hungry and irritable. We needed a big kill. I decided to head back to the meadow. I had not returned since winter set in and hoped the big grazers would seek out its rich grasses before it disappeared under a heavy layer of snow.

"Be careful, pup," Luke grumbled as he disappeared into the burrow. "Remember what I said about the two-legs. All animals are fleeing from them, predator and prey alike."

"I know, Luke," I said, exasperated. "I won't go far."

I could hear him grumbling but couldn't make out the words. Chuckling to myself, I took off toward the meadow. A light dusting of snow covered the ground and icicles hung from the trees. Cover would be difficult, but it meant the deer would be easy to spot.

Surrounding the meadow on three sides were the mountains, tall, imposing, snow-capped sentinels that separated the lush, fertile land from the harsh landscape beyond. Prey animals, like deer, understood the risk of entering the meadow but the temptation of rich food and crystalline water proved too strong. With winter fast approaching, deer needed all the rich food they could find. On this day, I was lucky.

A small herd of Whitetail grazed in the middle near the lake, one large buck and three doe. As I watched from the edge of the meadow, another buck ambled toward them. He was younger, and lame, heavily favoring his hind leg. From where I sat, it looked badly broken. Even without my intervention, he would not last through the winter. With my target chosen, I charged the herd.

The young buck collapsed even before I reached him, and I ended his struggle quickly. The rest of the herd disappeared into the trees. I looked over my kill. The buck was bigger than I realized and would feed Luke and I for days. Satisfied, I lifted my chin to call for my companion. Before the sound could leave my throat, I stopped. Luke wouldn't understand my call and it would only attract attention. Torn between eating or leaving my kill, I paced next to the deer. I remembered vividly what happened to the last meal I'd left unattended here. Luckily, there was enough, even for Swift, should the coyote beat me back.

Several yards away, at the edge of the meadow, was a cluster of bushes. It was my best chance to hide the carcass. With a great deal of effort, I managed to drag it the long distance and secured it under the thorny brush. Then, I ran to fetch Luke.

When I reached the burrow and called for him, he grumbled and bristled, either from being hungry or having his sleep interrupted. By now, I was used to his temper and just chuckled at him.

"I have food, my friend, but we'll have to go get it," I said.

"Well, lead on, then," he said, waving his paw at me.

I wanted to run back to the kill, but Luke's small legs couldn't keep up. Noticing my frustration, he told me to go on. He'd follow my tacks and meet up as soon as he could. Needing no further invitation, I ran ahead, eager to fill my belly.

When I reached the meadow, my eyes locked on the brush. I had a singular purpose, reach the kill and fill my empty belly. This one thought blinded me to the danger that awaited me. Just as I reached the brush, I heard it, a deep growl unlike any I'd heard before. I looked up just as the she-cat made to pounce.

The mountain lion was huge, easily bigger than me, and she came at me through the air with claws and teeth bared. I froze an instant too long, and she crashed into me. Together, we rolled in the snow, teeth, claws, and fur flying everywhere. I snarled and snapped at her, but I was poorly outmatched. If she clamped her teeth onto my neck, I was done for.

Her back legs dug into my belly as she kicked out. I yelped, feeling every claw dig into my flesh. Somehow, I managed to break free, and we stood, circling each other. Both sported injuries, mine more grievous than hers. Her feline eyes bore into me with a kind of insanity, and I realized she was scared. Not of me, but of something only she had been witnessed to. Before I could think further on it, she pounced again.

Once more, we were tangled in a struggle for life. Suddenly, we heard an ungodly racket and from the corner of my eye, I noticed Luke tearing through the snow. The she-cat paused long enough to look at the offender, and I broke free. Luke faced her, snarling and hissing. She backed off slightly, watching him with a mix of curiosity and trepidation. Eventually, she turned and headed back to the kill. I started to follow, not willing to give up my meal so easily.

"Let it go, pup," Luke said.

But I ignored him and charged after her anyway. With the ease only a cat could have, she turned at my charge and swiped her huge paw. It connected solidly against my shoulder, the claws shredding through fur and flesh and launching me several feet away. I landed heavily in the snow, the breath knocked from my lungs. She turned to finish the job, but Luke moved between us. With the fight won, she returned to the carcass.

"You alright, pup?" Luke asked.

"I can't believe I lost to a cat," I said, using humor to disguise my pain.

"Well, yur lucky I got here when I did. I told ya the predators were moving. Yur gonna have to be more careful."

"Gotcha," I grumbled, struggling to my feet.

"Come on, let's get ya cleaned up."

Chapter Eight: The Derby

Winter had fully claimed the land. Deep
snowdrifts covered the ground and the trees lay bare,
their skeletal limbs little cover for prey or predator.
My favorite place, my meadow, was no longer the
fertile, green utopia I remembered. Snow buried the

flowers and grass, and the lake lay sheathed under a heavy layer of ice. Even the birds, which gifted my sanctuary with song were long gone, seeking warmer climes. But this was my home, and I thrived in it.

Luke and I temporally went our separate ways. He chose to sit the winter out underground where he had plenty of food to get himself by. For my part, I sought out a land to call my own. I intended to keep the meadow and fan out from there. Fenrir's pack, while still close, had posed no more threat to me. Even the mountain lion which had nearly ended my journey had moved on, probably up into the mountains that surrounded it.

Deer moved in and out of my territory, as did the occasional buffalo herd. When I could, I took the chance to bring one down. Sometimes, I even called Swift and invited him to help, offering him a portion of the pickings. The first time I offered, he balked at my nerve.

"Come on, Swift," I pled. "Wouldn't you like to have deer instead of mice?"

"Do ya know how much work it is to bring down a deer?" he scoffed.

I stared at him, incredulous. "Umm...yeah, Swift. I've brought down a few myself."

"Then why do ya need my 'elp?"

"I don't. I just thought you'd like to eat better." *And actually earn a meal,* I thought.

"I'm going to regret this, aren't I."

"Of course not. It'll be great!"

The hunt went surprisingly well, and we brought down a big buck after an extensive chase. Swift lagged after I took the deer to the ground.

"Do you 'ave any idea how completely exhausted I am?" he panted, dragging himself across the snow.

I chuckled at his fallen shoulders and droopy ears. Before long, he joined me in eating and soon, our bellies were full. Afterward, we went our separate ways. Swift said he needed to go and 'sleep off his exhaustion, 'whatever that meant, and I left to re-establish my territory lines.

The next week slipped by quiet and peacefully. For once in over a month, the sun broke through the grey clouds, eventually banishing them altogether. A clear blue sky stretched above me, and I soaked in the little heat offered by the unobstructed sun. I made my way back to the meadow, wanting to see its glory under the sun's rays.

Suddenly, a sharp crack of thunder pierced the quiet of the forest. Its echo followed the sound of hundreds of birds as they took to the sky. I turned my head up to a bright blue sky without a cloud in sight.

"What was that?" I asked myself. A moment later, Swift plowed into me, terror streaked across his face.

"Run, Timbah!" he said, regaining his feet. "We 'ave to hide!"

"Why? What was that?" I follow him into the forest, trying to keep up with him in the thick underbrush.

"The two-legs call it a 'derby.' Once a year, for two days, they come into the forest and kill every wolf and coyote they can find, the bigger, the better. That sound was 'heir weapon. It can hit ya from a long way away, and ya won't even know it's comin'."

"That's awful!"

"It's what two-legs do."

As we raced through the forest, more shots reached my ears, some far away, and some close. After what seemed like an eternity, Swift scuttled down into a narrow hole. I looked at it skeptically, not fully confident my large size could squeeze through. Another shot, too close for comfort, had me testing my theory. After a great deal of wiggling, I managed to make it through. The passage opened once I was inside, and I was able to move more freely.

Swift curled up into a ball on a pallet of dried grass near the back of the burrow, his paws over his ears. He seemed terrified as I joined him. It felt weird to seek comfort from the one who had harassed me for so long, but some part of me knew we both needed it.

Swift and I jumped when the hunters fired their weapon close to the burrow. The cry of a wolf followed shortly after.

"Woo-hoo! I got it!" cried a hunter. The language was foreign and unfamiliar to me, but I knew I would never forget it. They moved on without noticing our hiding place, and Swift breathed a sigh of relief.

Throughout the night, and the following day, the forest echoed the hunters 'shots, occasionally followed by the cries of an animal. Whether wolf or coyote, it didn't matter. Every cry tore at my soul. By the night of the second day, the forest had fallen into an eerie silence. Against Swift's advice, I made my way to the entrance.

"Be careful, Timbah," he said. "They're still out there."

"Swift, is that how your mate died?" I asked.

I had considered it since the shooting began. His silence spoke volumes, and I turned to look at him. The pain in his eyes was all the answer I needed.

"How can they be so cruel?" Swift didn't answer and I turned again toward the entrance. "I need to call home and make sure my family is okay."

As I stepped out into the night, I was met with a dead calm so complete you could hear an acorn drop to the forest floor. The tracks in the snow told the story of the previous two days. Mud from too many hunters 'feet stained the pristine white and turned it to slush that seeped between my toes. I avoided the direction the hunters took. I didn't want first-hand knowledge of their carnage. Seeking out an area of high ground, I trudged up the slope.

From my vantage point, I could see a great distance. At first, the silence followed me. I'd never heard the forest so quiet. Lifting my chin, I called home. It was the first time I had done so since I left. I knew it was dangerous, but I had to know my family was okay.

My anxiety rose the more time that passed without a response. Finally, just as I was about to give up, I heard my father's howl. Joy soared through me. My mother's call followed soon after, followed one by one by the rest of the pack. Surprisingly, Thor and Zoe's call answered from a different direction, quite a way from my father's pack.

So, they did leave and form their own pack, I thought. *Good for them!*

Other calls began to echo the forest, not related to either pack. Tears sprang to my eyes at the sound. The hunters hadn't won. The packs were broken and scattered, but we were still alive. Fenrir's howl echoed close by, and I smiled. We may have been rivals but I was glad he was still alive.

The wolf calls seemed to bring the forest back to life and other animals began to sing again. Coyotes, who were usually solitary and quiet, even added to the song. A lone wolf call caught my attention. She was very close, and her cry was full of heartbreak and anguish. It pulled at my heartstrings and before I knew it, I was moving toward her.

An hour or so later, I found her. Fur as black as night, she curled into a ball on a rock, blending into the shadows. I looked around for her pack, but I instinctively knew they were gone, victims of the hunter's sport. I slowly made my way to her, whining softly to alert her of my presence. Her head shot up, and she turned wary eyes to me. They were golden, like my father's, and full of fright.

"Shh, I'm not going to hurt you," I said softly, slowly approaching her.

My ears and head were down in a non-threatening posture. I didn't want her to run off. She let me move toward her, watching me with cautious eyes. As I reached her, I touched my nose to hers. She lowered her head and whimpered, the sound tearing through me. I crawled up on the rock with her and curled my bulk around her much smaller frame.

"It's alright now," I assured her. "I'll protect you for now on."

I had found the beginning of my pack, and I was determined the hunters would no longer endanger those under my protection.

Chapter Nine: Game of Chance

The following few weeks, I scoured every inch of my land for signs of the hunters. With my territory being small, it didn't take long, and the task was easy. Unfortunately, it was also located close to the hunters' habitats. As other animals fled the two-legs, they traveled through my land. I did not harass them, as long as they kept moving. But I feared how close the hunters were getting.

The only place I felt was truly safe, was the meadow. It was defendable, provided a good source of food, water, and protection. And if we had to flee, we could do so through the mountains where the hunters were unlikely to follow. I brought Shilo with me. She wouldn't speak and had hidden within her grief. I knew with time, she would recover but for now, I was determined to take care of her.

Luke came to my aid, offering to help me dig out a den. Even Swift, although not his usual chirpy self, agreed to help. Before long, I had a large den, big enough for both Shilo and me. I settled her inside and left to find food. Swift sat outside the den when I exited.

"Thank-you, Swift," I said, sitting next to him.

"No worries," he said. "It's the least I can do. Now, ya got yur pack and yur territory. I expect great meals in the future."

The twinkle in his eye gave him away, and we both burst out laughing.

"You're hopeless," I said, nudging his shoulder.

"I know. But ya wouldn't want me any other way." He got to his feet and loped off into the trees.

I shook my head, chuckling as I went off in the opposite direction.

Shilo came out of her shell soon after, easily warming up to me. She was young, not even a full turn of the seasons, and her entire pack were victims of the hunters. I marveled at her fire and wit as she danced circles around me. Her spirit reminded me of Zoe, and I found myself laughing often. She was also very good at hunting, embarrassingly so. Together, we had no problem bringing down large prey.

But one thing still haunted her. She didn't want to be alone. The first time I left to check my territory, her fear nearly held me back.

"Timber don't do this. Please!"

"I have to, Shilo. If I don't, someone is going to get hurt."

"And if you do, you could get hurt."

"This is our land now. We must protect it and all those who live within it. It's my duty to ensure that everyone within these borders is safe. My father would do the same. Don't worry. I'll be fine." With one final nuzzle, I slipped from the den and headed for the trails.

The first sign you'll find is their scent, I remembered Swift telling me. *Two-legs can never hide their scent completely. Second, are their tracks. They bumble through the forest disruptin' leaves and branches. Third, they like to lay their traps on well-traveled paths, like trails to sources of water. The traps'll be covered with dead leaves and grass. Yu'll need some way to set them off without gettin' too close. If they get ya, it's all done, game over.*

It didn't take long for me to find the first signs of hunter activity. Luke had been right. They were on the move. I carefully made my way to the stream that ran through my small territory. Sure enough, the scent of two-legs overpowered me. I narrowed my eyes in the dim light of the forest trail. I couldn't make out anything in particular, but the forest was eerily quiet.

Bending down, I picked up a branch laying on the ground. *Here goes nothing,* I thought, as I tore down the center of the trail. The branch set off every trap it hit, the loud snap causing me to jump each time. After I'd reached the water, I turned and repeated the action on the other side. When I was done, I turned to study my handiwork. Although satisfied, I felt a chill race through my body at the sheer number of traps. Shaking it off, I headed back to Shilo.

I continued to disarm the traps scattered throughout my land for several days. So far, no one had been hurt, and I knew my efforts were worth it. As I made my way to the farthest reaches of my territory, I picked up a highly concentrated dose of the hunters 'scent. My curiosity got the better of me, and I left the safety of my territory.

I followed the scent quite a way before I found the source. A hastily built den of sorts sat nestled among the remains of several downed trees. The structure was unnatural with straight, angular walls. Along one side hung dried fish and a pail of old water. As I made my way around the building, something tugged at my tail, just enough to get my attention.

I whipped around, fearing I had been caught. Swift stepped back and shook his head.

"What is this?" I asked, turning back to the building.

Swift walked up and sat next to me. "This is the two-legs 'den. They tear down the forest to make it."

I looked around at the mess of dead branches and animal bones laying scattered on the ground. The smell of death and decay was so powerful, I was surprised the hunters could stand it. I made to circle the building again, but Swift stopped me.

"I would leave, if I were ya, Timbah," he said, continuing to sit where he was.

"What is it, Swift? What don't you want me to see?"

"Suit yurself. But don 'say I didn't warn ya." With that, he got to his feet and trotted off.

I reached the other side of the building and froze in my tracks. A smaller structure, the same shape as the building, sat against the wall. It stood taller than I on my hind legs and was filled to overflowing with skins. Wolf, coyote, bear, fox, and bobcat were the primary skins I could make out. More skins stretched across the wall of the building, drying in the sun.

I jumped back, snorting, and shaking my head in a vigorous attempt to dislodge the image from my mind. Now, I understood why it reeked of death and why the hunters seemed impervious to the smell. Biting back a cry, I turned and fled for home.

Along the way, I came up with different strategies for how I could get rid of the hunters. I missed Zoe at that time. She had a brilliant mind and always proved the better strategist. But I preferred her out of harm's way. I already had enough to worry about with Shilo.

As I made my way to the meadow, heavy black clouds rolled in. A storm was coming and from the looks of it, it was going to be massive. I took the time I had to hunt, managing to bring down a small, half-starved elk just outside the meadow. I dragged it back to the den and called for Shilo.

She came tearing out of the den and plowed into me, licking me from chin to crown. I chuckled at her exuberance.

"Hey, honey. I'm home," I said, returning her affections.

"You're late!" she teased, and turned her attention to the deer. "Well, at least you brought food. I guess I'll keep you around a little longer."

"Is that right?" I nuzzled her again before we dug into our meal.

When we'd had our fill, I dragged the carcass away from the den and joined Shilo inside. A few minutes later, the heavens opened. Heavy drifts of snow blew sidewise in the strong winds, piling up against rocks and trees. Before long, our den lay buried beneath several feet of snow. The sheer size and depth of the dwelling kept us from suffocating.

We curled up next to each other, warm and comfortable as the blizzard raged overhead. With full bellies, we wouldn't need to leave the den for days, which suited us just fine. I wanted to spend the time with my mate and not think of what I had witnessed that day or of what I would need to do once the storm stopped. Perhaps sensing my mood, Shilo cuddled closer, laying out beside me and rested her head on my paws.

"Sleep, love," I said gently, licking her snout. "All will be well soon."

"All is well now," she said. "I'm glad you're home in one piece."

"I will always come home to you," I promised. "No matter what."

"Good, I'll hold you to that."

"Would you like to hear a story?"

"About what?" She seemed intrigued and cracked her eye open.

"About my father and his many adventures. My father is a great storyteller, and he passed all his tales on to me."

"That's sounds like an excellent way to pass the time."

And so, I spent the next several days regaling Shilo with my father's exploits, and some of my own. I told her all about Luke and Swift and how I had met both. She seemed to thoroughly enjoy the tales about the coyote and found a humor in them that I seemed to have missed. I had her in stitches over his antics and she swore she'd have to meet him properly once the snow cleared. I told her he wasn't nearly as charming as I'd somehow made him out to be, but she insisted. A week after being snowed in, the storm blew itself out and we were finally able to dig ourselves free.

Chapter Ten: Gambit

As we emerged from the den, I knew the threat of the hunters was gone, at least temporarily. Huge snow drifts blanketed the world, even burying the lake under several feet of snow. Even I had a hard time finding my footing, let alone a two-legged hunter.

On top of that, it was bitterly cold. The moisture in the air formed crystals that glittered in the brilliant light of the sun, angel dust, my father had called it. As I breathed out, my breath created a cloud of vapor that seemed to go on forever.

I shook my head, creating a halo around me. It was going to be a cold few weeks, and we needed to find food. I turned to Shilo, who currently rolled around in the snow, and chuckled. When she got to her feet, she was nearly as grey as me. Shaking out her coat, she threw snow in every direction.

"Are you ready to hunt, love?" I asked.

"Always." And with that, she took off.

The rest of the winter passed with relative peace. The hunters did not return, and I expanded my territory to include most of Fenrir's old land. The older wolf had suffered at the hunters 'hand. His pack was only a fraction of what it once was, and he'd lost his mate during the derby. I ached for him, as much as I did all the other broken packs in the area.

Near the end of winter, I decided to revisit the hunter's den. I wanted to reclaim the territory and remind the hunters that this land did not belong to them; they could not simply come in and destroy everything I had worked so hard for. The difference now was, I'd be taking Shilo with me. We had been inseparable since the blizzard, and I wanted her to see the breadth of our land. I also wanted to teach her what Swift had taught me concerning hunter behavior and their trapping methods. My pack would not fall victim to the hunters 'games.

Shilo seemed eager to learn and listened attentively as we traveled our land. She soaked up knowledge like a sponge and absorbed everything I said as if it were air. I felt it, the moment she first scented the hunters. Even from behind me, I felt her bristle and stiffen. The scent was old, from before the blizzard so I knew we were safe. I encouraged her to follow me to the two-legs 'den.

To my relief, all signs of death and carnage were gone. The small structure which had held the skins was gone, as were the skins on the wall. All that was left was the building and an old ring of blackened wood. I approached the building and peered into the strange openings on the wall. It was empty, save for a few trinkets scattered on the edges of the floor. Making my mark, Shilo and I left to continue re-establishing our borders.

At our farthest border, closest to the two-legs' habitats, I noticed signs of recent activity. A new fence had been erected and I could hear a strange lowing in the distance. It sounded vaguely like that of the buffalo but not as deep. I turned back to Shilo, who shook her head adamantly. But I had to know what this new threat was.

"Timber!" she hissed. "Don't cross that wire! We can't go into the two-legs 'land."

"I just want to see what it is," I reassured her, nudging her chin.

"No, you don't! Trust me on this. Please!" Her golden eyes were wide with panic.

"Alright. Let's go home."

I turned away from the fence and followed her away, but my head turned back toward the mysterious sound. With my attention focused behind me, I failed to see the danger we were walking into. A loud snap brought my head around and I watched in slow motion as Shilo yelped and jumped into the air. The hunter's trap landed with a thud, the branch Shilo had pushed into it snapped in two.

"Don't move," I cried at her shaking frame.

I scanned the trail frantically, looking for signs of more traps. There was never just one trap. Sure enough, just beyond the one she had set off, were more hidden under old leaf litter. Why hadn't I noticed the hunters 'tracks before? The snow had begun to melt, and the forest floor was a mess of ice, snow, and slush. On this part of the trail, the slush had given way to freezing mud.

I turned my head, looking for a branch suitable for disarming the traps. The ground had no shortage of branches, victims of the harsh winter. I carefully made my way to a large one and picked it up, clamping it tightly in my teeth. Shilo watched me with worry. I knew she feared for me, and I made my way over to her. I dropped my branch and nuzzled her briefly.

"I know you're scared, but I need you to be brave," I said. "I have to set off these traps. It's going to be loud and frightening, but I need you to stay calm. Can you do that for me?"

She nodded her head and returned my affection. "Be careful," she whispered.

"I always am."

I picked the branch back up and ran down the trail. Shilo yelped as the first trap went off but held in her fear with the rest of them. The traps seemed to go on forever and by the time I reached the end, I could no longer see her. My thoughts were temporarily on other things, however. The last trap was not empty when I reached it. A rabbit had stumbled across it and paid with its life. My eyes burned with an anger I'd never felt before.

After several minutes, a soft brush along my side alerted me to Shilo's presence. I couldn't tear my eyes from the rabbit. Shilo pushed her nose against my shoulder and whimpered.

"You couldn't stop this," she soothed. "You are but one wolf. What could you have done?"

"Do you know how many wolves were killed in my father's pack after he established his own territory?"

"Timber, don't do this."

"None. Do you know why? Because he knew what to do. He knew how to avoid the hunters and keep the pack safe. My negligence nearly cost you your life today."

"But it didn't. How many have you saved by disarming these traps all winter? You see, Timber, your father moved away from the hunters when they became a threat and that's okay because he had the land to do so. But you stand your ground and refuse to give up. That makes you just as strong and brave as your father."

"This has to stop. From now on, I am taking my fight to the hunters. This is my gambit and with it, I openly declare war on the two-legs."

"What are you going to do?"

In answer, I started to dig at the posts holding the traps. Once freed, I dragged all of them to a hole I had dug and buried them. Let see how well the traps worked when the hunters couldn't find them. Exhausted, Shilo and I made our way home.

For the next week, I continued to disarm and bury the traps. Fortunately, the number seemed less and less, and I suspected the hunters were running out. I also imagined them frustrated.

Shilo continued to travel with me and became an expert at locating and disarming the traps. It was during this time the Swift reentered our lives. Shilo and I had just finished burying the last of the traps, and I stretched to loosen the tense muscles of my shoulders.

"'ello, love," I heard behind me.

Shilo yelped and jumped into me. Sighing, I turned to face him.

"Hello, Swift," I said. "It's been a while."

"Well, ya know. It's been cold. I haven't gotten out much. 'oo's yur friend?"

I rolled my eyes. Swift already knew who Shilo was but for some reason was playing dumb.

"This is Shilo, my mate," I said patiently, turning adoring eyes to her. "Shilo, this is Swift, my great annoyance."

"Hello, Swift," she said with a mysterious gleam in her eye. "I've heard quite a bit about you."

"Really? Timbah ne'er could keep 'is mouth shut. 'Course, I know deep down 'e cares. Why, this one time..."

I rolled my eyes and began the long trek home, followed by Swift and Shilo, who was engrossed in his storytelling. I tried to tune them out, but Swift's embellishments of his prowess were too much to bear. I turned around to correct his tale but stopped mid-way. Something didn't seem right.

"Shh!" I hissed and turned my head toward the setting sun.

Swift stopped abruptly, and we all three went on guard. After a few seconds, I heard the sound that had originally caught my attention, dogs. As one, we turned and ran. We had to reach the meadow, but I feared we'd never make it. We were too far away, and the dogs were too close.

"We need to split up," Swift said. "They can't chase all of us."

"It's too dangerous, Swift!" I barked. "Stay with us until we get to the den. We can wait the hunters out there."

"It'll be fine. Take yur mate to safety. I'll lead the two-legs off. No worries. They can't catch me!" With that, he veered off, barking and howling.

"That fool!"

Shilo glanced at me, worry clouding her own features. She was my singular purpose now. I had to protect her. A shot echoed the forest, and the birds overhead beat their wings into the sky. I stumbled in my run. *Swift!* No other shot came, and I feared for my friend. I fought past my anguish and continued. The sound of the dogs faded, and I breathed easier knowing Shilo and me were safe.

We slowed our frenzied run and moved into an easy lope. Neither spoke, both of our hearts too heavy for words. If I hadn't been so overcome with grief, I may have noticed the eerie quiet of the forest.

"Timber," Shilo whispered. "Something's wrong."

Before I could consider her words, the forest once again echoed the hunter's weapon. I felt an agonizing pain assault my flank, and Shilo yelp in terror. Before I knew it, we were racing again. I bit past my pain as it lanced down my leg and across my back. I had to hide Shilo. I couldn't save us both.

We passed a fallen tree with its huge roots pulled out of the ground. It was the best chance for hiding her.

"Stay here, love," I said, masking my pain. "You have to hide until the hunters are gone. I'll lead them away and come get you when it's safe."

"Don't leave, Timber!" she cried. "We can hide here together."

I shook my head before she even finished.

"They will track me to you." I turned and showed her my injury, my silver fur coated in red. "I will come for you. Stay safe."

I nuzzled her one last time and ran off. I managed to keep up my pace for several more minutes before my strength started to fail. I grew dizzy and stumbled through the brush. I vaguely remember crashing through a fence before passing out. The last sound to reach my ears was the scream of a two-legged child.

Chapter Eleven: Captive

I struggled with consciousness for what seemed like an eternity, stuck in some half-dazed state of awareness where nothing made any sense. Each time I woke, I was surrounded by two-legs. The pain in my rump had subsided, but I suspected that had more to do with my dazed state than anything else.

After some time, the haze wore off, and I opened my eyes to unfamiliar surroundings.

I lay in a structure with hard, unforgiving sides that reflected the dim light of the room. In front of me stood a wall which I could see through but not escape from. The room beyond was quiet, save for the few other animals that slept in similar structures.

I gingerly lifted my head to examine my wound. A piece of white fabric covered my flank, and my rear back leg was pulled up and secured snuggly against my belly. It was uncomfortable, and I ached to have it removed. I tried to reach the bandage but found I was still too weak for such activity.

At the far end of the room a door opened and light flooded in. Two two-legs entered, engrossed in some conversation I could not understand. They were covered, head-to-toe in white.

"Good, he's awake," one of them said, approaching me. "I can't believe he ran all that way on a broken hip."

"He's a tough one. I don't think I've ever seen a wolf this big before."

"Hey there, big guy," the first two-leg said, peering into my dark sanctuary. "You're okay now. In a few weeks, you'll be good as new."

She slid a bowl of water under the door. Despite my trepidation, I lapped at it hungrily. My throat burned with the need for water. They left soon after, taking the light with them. My life in captivity had just begun.

My sense of time in the two-legs' domain was untrustworthy, but I assumed I'd been locked in my cage for two weeks or more. My wound healed slowly and even after all that time, I still couldn't put weight on it. In fact, when I was let out to stretch my legs, the offending limb was kept tethered to my abdomen.

I came to learn the two-leg who had given me water was called Alex. She was kind and patient, and I began to enjoy it when she stroked me behind the ear. She brought me everything I needed and often read out loud late into the night. This was how I gained a rudimentary understanding of their language. Shortly after coming to the sanctuary, she decided I needed a name.

"In the land of my people, wolves are worshipped and revered," she said, holding what she called a book full of pictures. "The brave warriors of our tribe endeavored to be like the wolf: strong, fierce, brave, and unfailingly loyal to their families. You remind me of those warriors. You are *ohitika*, brave, and you are *shunkaha*, wolf. Your coat is *maza ska*, silver. So, I will call you *shunkaha ohitika maza ska,* brave silver wolf, or *Tika*, for short. What do you think?"

I stuck my nose through the bars and licked her hand. It really didn't matter what she called me. I just wanted to go home. In time, Alex took me to an exercise yard. It was surrounded by a high fence and forest beyond. I would spend the next several weeks in this enclosure, a mockery to freedom. The first night she left me out, melancholy hit heavy in my

117

heart. Before I could consider the consequences, I lifted my head and howled. I poured all my anguish into the call. The answer I received confirmed my fears. I did not recognize any of the wolves who called back. I must have been a long way from home if I could not reach familiar voices.

As I made to curl up and sleep away my heartache, a call did reach me. She was so far away that I barely heard her. Shilo! I stood to call back but thought better of it. I didn't want her to get caught as well. With my spirits lifted, I went to sleep.

The next few weeks were brutal. Alex deemed my hip mostly healed and wanted me to start rebuilding the muscle. She stretched my leg and turned it this way and that. It hurt and if not for the other two-legs holding me down, I probably would have snapped at her. Eventually, she worked out the soreness and I was able to put some weight on it. Then, the real work began.

She called me an "ambassador" and said it was up to me to show other two-legs that wolves weren't dangerous. I think she also wanted to show me that not all two-legs were monsters. Twice a day, she would take me in front of a huge crowd of two-legs, most of them young, and talk about what it means to be a wolf and how we were important to the environment.

My first time frightened me, and I cowered behind her. It didn't take long before I became comfortable around the younglings. They reminded me of wolf cubs, full of energy and wonder with eyes wide and curious. By the end of the first week, I was comfortable with them rubbing my fur.

"Wolves are a keystone species," Alex said, addressing thirty or so children sitting rapt in the audience. "Does anyone know what this means?"

A girl in the front raised her hand and Alex pointed to her. "A keystone species is one that other species depend on, like wolves to deer."

"That's very good! Most predators are considered keystone species because they keep the balance of nature. Wolves hunt deer, usually sick or injured ones, which keep herds manageable and healthy. What happens if the wolves are no longer around and there is nothing to hunt the deer?"

This time a boy raised his hand. "The deer will become sick and will not have enough food to feed them all."

"Excellent answer! We see this now in our southern states where feral hogs compete with native wildlife for food. Wolf kills provide not only food for themselves but for a host of other animals as well, in the form of scavengers. These include eagles, bears, foxes, and many species of birds.

"Since the reintroduction of grey wolves to Yellowstone, a balance has returned. Trees, such as Willow, can flourish now that the Elk no long eat them. Beavers, which rely on Willow branches, have also grown in number. With beavers, come ponds, which bring insects, fish, amphibians, reptiles, birds, mammals, and moose. Can you see now, why wolves are considered a keystone species?"

Alex continued to teach the young two-legs about me and my family, from our family structures to our complicated role in nature. I found it surprising she understood us so well. If she knew, then others must as well. I looked around at the rapt audience soaking in her every word and beyond them, adult two-legs who I assumed to be their parents. How could the hunters be so cruel if people understood us the way Alex did? Perhaps the hunters just didn't understand.

I looked up at Alex as she became animated with her story, using her weak voice to try and simulate a howl. I took pity on her and did it for her. The audience cheered and clapped after my performance, and Alex beamed down at me. I felt her joy in my heart and suddenly, I understood what she was doing. She was championing my cause and that of all wolves in the wild.

"Say good-bye to *Tika*," she said, finishing her demonstration.

All thirty-plus younglings called, "Bye-bye, *Tika!*"

"Good job," Alex said as the two-legs filed out.

As she led me back to my enclosure, I heard a familiar howl off in the distance. It wasn't Shilo, but my sister, Zoe. I wondered how she had found me. I called back to her throughout the evening. Late into the night, she emerged from the forest, followed closely by Thor. My heart leapt at the sight of her, and I hopped over to the fence. Sticking my nose through the holes we shared what affection we could.

"Timber, what have you gotten yourself into?" she asked, tears in her voice.

"Just a little run-in with the hunters. I'm almost completely healed. What are you doing here?"

"We heard your calls and have been searching for you ever since. Father is worried sick."

"I'm sorry I worried you all." I turned to Zoe's mate. "Hello, Thor. Thank-you for taking care of my sister."

"She is the one who takes care of me," he said affectionately.

"We need to get you out of here," Zoe said, digging at the bottom of the fence.

"Don't Zoe. I can't go yet."

She stopped and stared at me. "Why not?"

"Because I can't run. I can barely walk." I turned to show her the bare patch on my flank where the fur was just starting to regrow. "Maybe in a couple more weeks but right now, I'd never make it far."

"We can't just leave you here, Timber."

"Zoe, I'll be fine. The two-legs are taking good care of me and as soon as I'm healed, I'll come home. But I need you to do something for me."

"Anything," Thor said, coming closer to the fence.

"My mate is still out there and she's all alone. Her name is Shilo. Can you protect her until I get out?"

"Of course. She'll be safe with us."

"Thank-you. I'll come find you as soon as I can."

Zoe nuzzled me once more before turning to go. Thor followed the motion and together, they disappeared into the trees. Soon after, I heard their calls as they searched for my mate. Her answering call was reassuring, and I knew before the night was over, they would be together.

Chapter Twelve: Homeward Bound

For three more weeks, Alex worked with me. I spent the morning learning how reuse my leg and the afternoons teaching. A few times, Alex even took us on road trips. The experience was not something I'd soon forget. The motion of the vehicle left my limbs feeling rubbery for some time after stopping.

She took me to places with different animals, all behind fences or enclosures. It seemed a sad existence to me, but the animals appeared fine with it. I walked with a slight limp close at her side and took in all the sights, both human and animal alike.

Alex called it a zoo and said it was a place where animals went when they couldn't survive in the wild. For one heart-stopping moment, I thought she'd brought me because my leg would never heal completely. Somehow sensing my anxiety, she scratched me behind my ears.

"This is no place for you, *Tika*," she comforted. "Soon, you will be going home where you belong." I basked in her words, more than ready to be reunited with my mate. After a presentation at the zoo, Alex carted us back to the sanctuary. I would have one more week before I was deemed fit enough to return to the wild.

My last day with Alex was bittersweet. On the one hand, I missed my wild home. The forest tugged at my longing, and I ached to stretch my legs once again. On the other hand, I'd formed a strong bond with Alex. I fantasized that she was a wolf in a past life. As we made our way to the truck, she slipped a heavy collar over my neck and fastened it securely.

"This way, we can always find you," she said, burying her fingers in my thick fur. "You stay safe, *Tika*, and steer clear of the hunters."

I licked her nose to show I understood, and she laughed. With the help of another human, she picked me up and set me in a large crate, the same one I'd used when visiting the zoo. She secured it and they closed the vehicle door. I could hear them speaking from the other side.

"Where did you want to release him?" The male asked. "You know they found him on the edge of human settlements."

"I know. We can't take him back there. I don't want him anywhere near hunting grounds."

"You could take him to Yellowstone. He'd be protected there."

"You're right. And it's far enough away that he can start over. I'll see you when I get back."

I wasn't going home. Laying down, I curled in a ball. How long would it take me to find my way home? The truck started and rolled onto the gravel drive. During the long drive, my mind was focused on one thing, finding my way home.

Several hours later, the truck finally came to a stop. Alex exited and left to talk to another human. A few minutes later, she returned, followed by whoever she had been talking to. Together, they lowered my crate to the ground.

"Good-bye, *Tika*," she said. "I'm really going to miss you."

She stood and opened the door of my crate. For two whole seconds I stood frozen, staring at the unobscured view of my new home. And then I was gone, stretching my legs as far as they would go to cover as much ground as I could. After a few minutes, I slowed to a stop and looked back at Alex.

She swiped at her eyes and waved. Just for her, as a way to say good-bye, I lifted my chin and howled.

Now to find Zoe. I ran all day and long into the night in the direction I believed to be home. Every now and then, I would rest and call home. But every call echoed back without an answer. I refused to give up and continued my journey, stopping only long enough to rest and fill my belly.

A week later, I was beginning to get discouraged. I collapsed next to a river, lapping up the cool water. Summer had come with a vengeance and my thick coat trapped the heat from all my running. After quenching my thirst, I collapsed on my side.

"Are you alright?" a voice asked above me.

I looked up to see a kestrel perched in the tree over my head. "Yes," I answered. "I'm just trying to find my way home."

"Where are you headed?"

"A meadow, surrounded on three sides by mountains with a crystal-clear lake in the center."

"I've seen that meadow," the bird said, dropping down next to me. He was small and colorful, with a blue-capped head and red back. "I'll show you the way."

I jumped up, suddenly reenergized. "Thank-you…"

"Haji. And it's no problem. I was lost once, too."

"Thank-you, Haji. I'm Timber."

"It's nice to meet you, Timber. Now, let's get you home."

I followed him into the night and most of the next day. By evening of the second night, we were both exhausted. Haji perched on my back as I stood catching my breath. We stopped on a cliff facing a wide expanse of grasslands.

"Cross this valley and continue into the forest on the other side," he said. "You'll be able to see your mountains soon after. Head for them. Within a couple of days, you should reach your meadow."

"I can't thank you enough, Haji."

"Think nothing of it. Do you mind me asking why you were so far from home?"

"I was injured by a hunter. After I healed, the two-legs took me somewhere they thought was safe. But it wasn't my home, and I have family waiting for my return."

"Looks like we have something in common. A few years back, I was shot from the sky. Two-legs helped me, too." He ruffled his feathers. "Good luck in the future."

"Thanks. You, too."

He jumped into the air and flew back the way he'd come, disappearing into the shadows. I turned back to the valley. I still had a long way to go but with renewed hope, I lifted my head and howled. No answer came, but I moved with a lighter step. I pushed my exhaustion aside and descended the cliff.

The valley took me three days to cross but it provided an abundance of food. I filled up on mice and rabbits as I made my way through the tall, golden grass. During the day, when the heat was highest, I rested in whatever shade I could find. When the sun set, I resumed my journey. By the end of the third day, I reached the edge of the forest.

A creek flowed just inside the tree line, and I rushed to it. One thing the valley hadn't provided was water and I was parched. I filled my belly and crossed into the trees. It took a moment to get my bearings, and then I was off again.

By midday, I glimpsed my mountains. I headed straight for them, my eyes locked on their location. When the sun set, I stopped just long enough to call home again. Finally, I was rewarded with the sound I'd longed for. My father answered my call. After some time, other calls followed. I could not yet hear Zoe or Shilo, but I knew it was only a matter of time.

I continued my journey the next morning after a full night of rest. I did not stop again until the following night. By then, I could clearly make out the mountains that surrounded my meadow. Just one more day. I called for Zoe, and she answered soon after. To my utter joy, Shilo echoed my call. She sounded relieved and happy. I slept well that night with the knowledge we would soon be reunited.

The next morning, I rose early and raced the final leg of my journey. I had a singular purpose and every muscle in my body worked toward it. My legs stretched long and wide, covering great distances with each stride, and my chest heaved with each breath I took. The forest floor echoed the sound of my feet as they kicked up dirt and leaves. I knew the moment I crossed into my land, even though my scent had long dissipated. I felt it, all the way to my bones, as my land welcomed me home.

The meadow greeted me as I broke through the tree line, just as I first remembered it, green and lush. Shilo, sensing me, exited the den and watched as I tore across the ground. She ran to meet me, whimpering and wagging her tail. We collided in a tumbling ball of silver and black fur, licking each other's faces to reaffirm our bond.

Zoe and Thor stood a short distance away, nuzzling up to each other. I flashed them a look of gratitude before turning my attention back to Shilo. Thor nodded and he and Zoe turned, heading back to their own territory. I guided Shilo back to the den. After my long journey, I was exhausted.

As we entered the den, I had my greatest surprise yet. Swift stretched and yawned as he got his feet, perfectly healthy and whole.

"You little rascal!" I cried. "How on earth did you get away?"

"I told ya, two-legs can't catch me. I'll let ya get reacquainted. See ya around, Timbah. And welcome back."

My world had settled back into order, and I couldn't be happier. With Shilo by my side and my friends and family close, everything was as it should be. I curled up with Shilo and chuckled to myself. What a journey this had been!

"I'm back, love," I said as I nuzzled Shilo's ear.

"Welcome home, Timber."

Conservation Efforts

With the recent delisting of grey wolves, they are once again threatening extinction. In the past few years, studies done by Fish and Wildlife Services have concluded that grey wolves are no longer threatened with extinction. However, there are several flaws in the reports. One, they account for all wolves in North America, to include an abundant population in Canada and Alaska. Two, the studies do not consider the area where the wolves live. They need large territories to thrive, but many are isolated in small pockets in states like Montana, Idaho, and Wyoming. Conservationists who have worked so hard to rebuild the wild wolf population are crying out:

> "A 'pack' of wolves is not a snarling aggregation of fighting beasts, each bent on fending only for itself, but a highly organized, well-disciplined group of related individuals or family units, all working together in a remarkably amiable, efficient manner." (Holleman, 2013)

Marybeth Holleman, a contributor for *Writers on the Range*, tells a chilling story of the effects of wolf hunting. Not only is the ecosystem disrupted, but the overall health of wolf family units are as well. After extensive studies, biologist Gordon Haber found that some wolf packs who lost a significant number of members, or one or both alpha pair, fell into disarray which led to the deaths of many, if not all, of the rest of the pack. (Holleman, 2013)

In a healthy environment, wolf mortality is already high with few wolves living past six years. For dispersed wolves, those without a pack, the mortality rate is much higher. By breaking up solid family units, packs struggle to survive. Human hunting has escalated this problem. Most of the wolves hunted are "trophy" wolves. This almost always means the alpha pair. While Fish and Wildlife consider the wolves killed each year by humans, they neglect to account for those that die afterward when they can no longer survive on their own.

In addition to traditional riffle hunting, many states allow the use of inhumane wolf traps and hunting dogs. These are brutal techniques that prologue the suffering of wolves and add an unfair advantage to human hunters. The traps also capture animals other than wolves. ("Refuge From Cruel...")

What is the "derby?"

While the "derby" in this work is fictitious, it is based on the real-life, and highly controversial sport competition that was held in Salmon, Idaho this year. The derby, sponsored by Idaho for Wildlife, was billed "fun and wholesome entertainment for the entire family" by the anti-predator organization. In a two-day competition, hunters were encouraged to kill as many wolves and coyotes as they could, with prizes going to the largest wolf and most female coyotes killed. Competitors as young as 10 were allowed to participate. The hunt was unregulated, and participants did not need permits. (Fox, 2013)

Idaho is not alone in this wanton slaughter. More than 15 other such contest occur throughout the country targeting other predators like coyotes, foxes, and bobcats. The animals, listed as "non-game" by state wildlife agencies, are subjected to ruthless persecution that is not monitored. (Fox, 2013)

Idaho Commissioner, Larry Shoen had this to say:

"Shooting contests conducted in the name of killing animals for fun, money, and prizes is just not consistent with the values of most people in the modern world." (Fox, 2013)

What's Being Done

With the help of Conservation groups like the Wolf Conservation Center, Project Alpha Wolf, the Ian Somerhalder Foundation, and many, many more, we can raise awareness to the wolf's plight. Even though most of the citizens of the affected states disapprove of wolf delisting, the hunts continue, killing an average of 300 wolves a year in each state. How long would it take before North America's wolves are once again in danger?

In addition to public hearings, state representatives, like Rep. Nita Lowey from New York, are making a stand. She has introduced the bill, "Refuge from Cruel Trapping Act (H.R. 3513)" which, if passed, will end the use of certain types of traps. Additionally, Arizona's Rep. Raúl M. Grijalva has written a letter co-signed by 85 Democratic and Republican colleagues calling for the continued protection of grey wolves.

Wolf Conservation Center

The wonderful people of the WCC have contributed a great deal to the research for my book. With their daily updates and up-to-date information on local delisting hearings, I was able to keep abreast of the current situation, to include the highly endangered wild red wolves of North Carolina (less than 20 and falling) and Mexican grey wolves, "lobos" (less the 300 and slowly growing). Founded in 1999, the WCC is a private, not-for-profit organization dedicated to "promoting wolf conservation by teaching about wolves, their relationship to the environment, and the human role in protecting their future." (WCC)

http://nywolf.org
https://www.facebook.com/nywolforg

A community of like-minded animal lovers wishing to protect wolves and their natural world.

"As a group we feel that through public education, supporting existing organizations, and a place for some occasional comic relief, we can give the wolves a fighting chance in their struggle to survive." (P.A.W.)

http://projectalphawolf.wordpress.com/about/
https://www.facebook.com/ProjectAlphaWolf

An organization created by actor Ian Somerhalder in an effort to preserve the planet and all those who live in it.

"We are a team, a group of people, who view the environment as an interconnected organism of which we are not separate but a part of. There is no differentiation between all living things: trees, rivers, animals, and humans. We are all one interdependent organism." (ISF)

http://www.isfoundation.com/welcome

How You Can Help

As always, getting involved, spreading awareness, and education are key to the survival of wolves in the wild. There is a wealth of information to be found on the sites I have listed here, as well as how you can help, from signing petitions to donating, every little bit helps. Don't think that one voice alone can't make a difference because when one voice alone becomes many, we can make a difference. For continued updates, visit Nature's Guardians on our Facebook page (https://www.facebook.com/n.guardians) or our website (https://www.NaturesGuardiansBookSeries.com).

If you would like more information about WCC, P.A.W., ISF, or any of the other groups listed in this book, I encourage you to visit their websites. There are also many more organizations that I did not list. Please help us to make a difference.

Wolf Angels:
https://www.facebook.com/pages/Wolf-Angels/274653705499

White Wolf Pack:
http://www.whitewolfpack.com

References:

Fox, C. (2013 Dec. 23). "Two-Day Holiday Killing 'Derby' in Idaho Targets Wolves and Coyotes." Retrieved from http://www.huffingtonpost.com/camilla-fox/twoday-holiday-killing-de_b_4471553.html?

Holleman, M. (2013). "Holleman: Gray Wolves Betrayed by U.S. Fish and Wildlife Service Decision" Retrieved from http://www.summitdaily.com/news/8780038-113/wolves-family-haber-wolf

Grijalva, R. & et. al. personal communication, (11 Dec. 2013). Retrieved from http://grijalva.house.gov/uploads/Grijalva%20Letter%20to%20Jewell%20on%20Protecting%20Gray%20Wolves%20Dec.%2012.pdf

"Refuge From Cruel Trapping Act." Retrieved from https://www.facebook.com/photo.php?fbid=10151821708207635&set=a.121327847634.104946.117336407634&type=1&theater

Sahara's Plight

Nature's Guardians Series Book 3
(excerpt)

Chapter One: Spring

The first thing you notice about Africa in spring is all the green for as far as the eye can see. Tiny wildflowers dot an ocean of swaying green grasses like stars in the night sky. The bellowing of water buffalo and wildebeest mingle with the braying of zebra in a song to the season. Morning dew glistens like diamonds on flower petals and blades of grass. The dawn is filled with puffs of clouds snorted from the grazers, even as the sun struggles to rise from the darkness.

It is this world I was born into, me and my four siblings. I felt the tremble of the earth before I could either see or hear. The great beasts shook the earth as they moved across the plains. I slept, comforted by my mother's warm body and those of my siblings. Before long, my eyes opened onto a world I would soon be part of.

My mother chose her den well. We were ensconced in the hollow of a hill, probably an abandoned burrow of some other creature. From the top of the hill, she had a great vantage point, able to see far into the vast grassland that surrounded us. This afforded her the ability to spot prey that would otherwise be hidden.

Although she raised us alone, she provided for our every need, and I can't remember ever going hungry in those early days. By the time my siblings and I were a few weeks old, we had fallen into a routine: wake, nurse, play, and sleep. My brother, N'dugu, however, always tried to be different. From the beginning, his adventurous nature got him into trouble. I lost count of how many times Mother scolded him for trying to follow her out of the burrow.

When we were just a few months old, N'dugu's adventures became ours. We abandoned our safe burrow and followed Mother into the deep grass. As little as we were, we could not see above our hiding place, and the noises that reached us left me wondering what creature made the sounds. My mother's presence was a comfort to me. I knew she would protect us. The further we ventured from our burrow, however, the more we traveled into the unknown. Little did we know of all the dangers we would face in the weeks to come, and not all of us would make it through.

"N'dugu!" I cried for the hundredth time. "You know Mother said not to leave the brush."

My oldest brother sighed and turned to me. "Geez, Sahara. I'm just taking a peek. Nothing will happen, and if you don't say anything, Mother will never know."

"You can't keep disobeying her," I said, walking over to him. "You put us all in danger."

"Have you even seen these 'monsters' Mother speaks of?" he asked. "She only says that so we will do what she says."

"I don't have to see them. I can hear them."

N'dugu wouldn't listen. He never did. So, against our mother's wishes, he made his way to the edge of our hiding place. Before he could catch a glimpse of what lay beyond, Mother poked her head inside, her eyes narrowed. She glared down at him from her impressive height. In response, N'dugu smiled as only a cheetah could, flashing his needle-sharp baby teeth in mock innocence.

"Hello, Mother," he said, sitting on his haunches. His wild baby hair fluffed out around him, making for a comical picture. "I was just coming to greet you. How was the hunt?"

Mother closed her eyes and sighed. "N'dugu, one of these days..."

Mother said this every time N'dugu did something to disappoint her. We always wondered what came after that phrase, but she never finished it. Instead, she lifted him up by his scruff and carried him back to where the rest of us rested. I could see the indignation on his face and tried hard not to laugh. It was the least he deserved.

Mother laid down with N'dugu still in her jaws. He struggled to get away as soon as she released some of the pressure, but she pulled him back with a massive paw. To his ultimate horror, she began to clean him, her rough tongue smoothing the tawny fur of his back.

144

"Mom, this is embarrassing!" he cried. "I can do it myself."

Mother just ignored him and continued with her cleaning. Resigned, N'dugu flipped over onto his back and sighed. Mother, oblivious to his dramatic act, began cleaning the spotted fur of his belly. I couldn't hold back my laughter any longer. My chuckles emboldened my other siblings, and they followed my lead.

Without missing a beat or even looking our way, Mother said, "I don't know why you're laughing. You're next."

N'dugu smirked as our laughter stopped, and we ran to find hiding places. Well, most of us ran. My youngest sibling and only sister, Nahi, looked forward to alone time with Mother and waited patiently for her to finish with N'dugu. Nahi was the smallest of us, only half as big as N'dugu, who was the largest. She was also quiet and shy, preferring solitude to group activities. N'dugu, surprisingly, was very protective of her and helped her when she fell behind. His tenderness for our youngest sibling surprised me.

Mother gave N'dugu a final swipe of her tongue and released him. He shook his body and ran off, rolling in the dirt near Nahi. Mother beckoned Nahi closer, and the little cub went willingly into Mother's arms.

For the next few weeks, we traveled through the tall grasses, mother leaving occasionally to find food. We fell into a new routine, and life was once again comfortable. It was during this time that I noticed something strange about N'dugu. Not only was he more adventurous than the rest of us, but his appearance was changing as well. Mother had pebble-sized spots all over her body with smaller ones on her head and legs. This, she told us, was to allow her to blend in with the tall grasses. Me and my siblings all shared this trait, discounting the mane of tawny fur down our backs.

N'dugu, however, had splotches instead of spots and his tail had broad bands around it verses the spots on ours. Most interesting were the three stripes that ran down his back from his head to his tail. While his baby mane had hidden this, it was beginning to show the older he grew. Curious, I approached Mother one night while everyone else slept.

"Sahara, we are moving again tomorrow," she scolded lightly. "You should be sleeping."

"Mother, why does N'dugu look different than the rest of us?"

Mother looked at me closely, as though she were looking for something only she could see. After a quick glance at my sleeping siblings, she beckoned me closer. I curled up next to her, and she began her explanation.

"Sahara, when you are a bit older and can see the world as I do, you will notice that our kind are disappearing from the land. There are too many predators and not enough room. The lions and hyena are claiming the most fertile lands for themselves, away from the two-legs, which leaves us much too close to them. The two-legs fear us and believe that we hunt their animals. Because of this, they hunt us. Now, there are too few of us left."

She paused for a moment to gather her thoughts and continued. "Some believe there is a savior coming, a cheetah who will lead us to a better place where we are not hunted and can live in peace. This 'king" will stand out from the rest of us. He will be courageous, strong, and wise. With his guidance, we will once again have our place on the plains.

"Even the two-legs have their legends concerning this king. They call him *nsuifisi*– hyena leopard, because of the unusual markings on his fur. They fear him because they do not know what his arrival means. It is possible that your brother is this king cheetah."

I thought about what she said but could not imagine N'dugu as anything other than my disobedient and adventurous brother. Needing to speak my thoughts, I looked up at Mother.

"Do you really think N'dugu is wise," I asked.

The look on my face must have shown my skepticism because Mother simply chuckled. She gave me an affectionate nudge before answering my question.

"I think N'dugu has a lot of growing up to do. Perhaps one day he will surprise us all. Now, run along and get some sleep."

Shaking my head in disbelief, I did as she bid and returned to my siblings, curling up among them. With my mind filled with fantastical visions, I drifted off to sleep.

Also Available:

This collector set includes an autographed copy of the book (*Haji's Fight for Freedom*), a collectable falcon from Wild Republic w/ authentic bird calls, and an adoption certificate.

Haji's Fight for Freedom

Follow Haji in this coming-of-age story about a young falcon trying to find his way in the world. Facing the death of his father at the hands of humans and then abandoned by his mother, Haji's only solace lies in the companionship of his brother, Koru. But when Koru leaves with his life-mate, Haji finds himself alone. Soon after, the same humans who killed his father, return. Find out what happens when Haji is shot from the sky!

Collection can be purchased on the Nature's Guardians website: https://www.naturesguardiansbookseries.com/

The *Timber's Gambit* collection set includes an autographed copy of the book, an 8" collectable plush (through Wild Republic), and an adoption certificate. It can also be purchased through the Nature's Guardian website (listed above).

Sahara's Plight

Growing up on the plains of Africa is anything but easy. Sahara faces lions, starvation, and an encroaching human population. With space a valuable and limited resource, Sahara must fight tooth and nail to survive the harsh African wilderness. After a crippling lion attack, she is taken in by conservationists. Declaring

her unfit to return to the wild, they send her off to a European zoo where she must learn to fit in. Unable to do so, she faces death. Fortunately, one conservationist is on her side. Together, they make a mad dash back to Africa where she is reunited with her brother, N'dugu.

The *Sahara's Plight* collection set includes an autographed copy of the book, an 8" collectable plush (through Wild Republic), and an adoption certificate.

M'vita's Struggle

Having a big family means never wanting for anything. You have protection, loyalty, friendship, and affection. Most of all, you're never alone. But what happens if all of that is taken away?

M'vita was born into a large wild dog family, one of the largest ever seen. But when disaster strikes, she finds herself all alone, the sole survivor in a land of paradise without a single wild dog in sight.

Now, she has to find a way to survive and cope with her loneliness. Squaring off against predators three times her size, she comes to terms with her new role and makes unlikely allies in order to survive. After confiding her fears to an equally lost cheetah, will she finally find what she has been searching for?

About the Author

Alisha M Risen-Kent lives at home with her four children and cat in Texas where she loves working in her garden. Her passions are reading, writing, drawing, and photography and often creates all the artwork for her books. She is also an avid player of Dungeons & Dragons© and comes up with most of her story ideas from the campaigns she plays in. An advocate for conservation efforts, she often volunteers where she can to help rehabilitate injured animals. She is also strong in her faith and believes that God has a plan for everything.

www.ingramcontent.com/pod-product-compliance
Lightning Source LLC
Chambersburg PA
CBHW060515290526
45791CB00001B/401